THE
MILLIONAIRE'S
PATH

PASSION, OPTIMISM, AND WEALTH

MARK FISHER
with Marc Allen

BARNES
&NOBLE
BOOKS
NEW YORK

Published by MJF Books
Fine Communications
322 Eighth Avenue
New York, NY 10001

The Millionaire's Path
ISBN 1-56731-413-9

Manufactured in the United States of America on acid-free paper

MJF Books and the MJF colophon are trademarks of Fine Creative Media, Inc.

QM   10 9   8   7   6   5   4   3   2

THE INSTANT
MILLIONAIRE

CONTENTS

CHAPTER ONE

*In which the young man
consults a wealthy relative*

T HERE WAS ONCE a bright young man who
wanted to get rich. He had had his fair share
of disappointments and setbacks, it couldn't
be denied, and yet he still believed in his
lucky star.

While he waited for fortune to smile, he worked as
an assistant to an account executive in a small adver-
tising agency. He was inadequately paid and had felt
for some time that his job offered him little satisfac-
tion. His heart was simply no longer in it.

He dreamed of doing something else, perhaps
writing a novel that would make him wealthy and
famous and end his financial problems once and for

all. But wasn't his ambition a bit unrealistic? Did he really have enough talent and technique to write a bestseller, or would the pages be filled with the bleak, unfocused ramblings of his inner misery?

His job had been a daily nightmare for more than a year. His boss spent most of each morning reading the newspaper and writing memos before disappearing to indulge in a three-hour lunch. He also changed his mind continually and gave contradictory orders.

But it wasn't only his boss—he was surrounded by colleagues who were also fed up with what they were doing. They seemed to have abandoned any sense of vision; they seemed to have given up altogether. He didn't dare tell any of them about his fantasy of dropping everything and becoming a writer. He knew they would treat it as a joke. When he was at work he often felt cut off from the world, as if he was in a foreign country, unable to speak the language.

Every Monday morning he wondered how on earth he was going to survive another week at the office. He felt totally alienated from the files piled high on his desk, from the needs of clients clamoring to sell their cigarettes, their cars, their beer. . . .

He had written a letter of resignation six months

earlier and had walked into his boss's office a dozen times with the letter burning in his pocket, but he had never been quite able to go through with it. It was funny; he would not have hesitated three or four years ago, but now he seemed unsure of what to do. Something was holding him back, some kind of force— or was it simply cowardice? He seemed to have lost the nerve that had always helped him get what he wanted in the past.

He kept waiting till the time was ripe, finding all kinds of excuses for not jumping into action, wondering if he could ever really succeed. Had he turned into a perpetual dreamer?

Did his paralysis spring from the fact that he was saddled with debts? Or was it because he had simply started to get old, a process inevitably triggered the minute we give up our visions of the future?

One day, when he was feeling especially frustrated, he suddenly thought of visiting an uncle of his who had become a millionaire. Perhaps he might be able to give him some advice, or better yet, some money.

His uncle was a warm, friendly person who immediately agreed to see him. He refused to lend him any money, however, claiming he wouldn't be doing him a favor.

"How old are you?" his uncle asked, after listening to his tale of woe.

"Thirty-two," the young man whispered timidly.

"Do you know that by the time John Paul Getty was twenty-three he'd already made his first million? And that when I was your age, I had half a million? So how in the world is it that you are forced to borrow money at your age?"

"Beats me. I work like a dog, sometimes over fifty hours a week...."

"Do you really believe that hard work is what makes people rich?"

"I... I guess so... anyway, that's what I've always been led to believe."

"How much do you make a year—$25,000?"

"Yeah, about that much," replied the young man.

"Do you think that someone who earns $250,000 works ten times as many hours a week as you do? Obviously not! So if this person earns ten times more than you do without working any more than you do, then he must be doing something quite different from you. He must have a secret you are totally unaware of."

"That must be true."

"You're lucky you understand that at least. Most people don't even get that far. They're far too busy trying to earn a living to stop and think about how they could get rid of their money problems. Most people don't even spend an hour of their time trying to figure out how they could get rich and why they've never managed to do so."

The young man had to admit that, despite his burning ambition and his dream of making a fortune, he had never taken the time to really think his situation through. Everything seemed to distract him, and prevent him from facing up to a task that was obviously of fundamental importance.

The young man's uncle was silent for a while, then smiled.

"I've decided to help you out. I'm going to send you to the man who helped me get rich. He's called the Instant Millionaire. Have you heard of him?"

"No, never," the young man said.

"He chose that name because he claims he became a millionaire overnight after discovering the true secret of making a fortune. He claims he can help anyone become a millionaire overnight—or at least acquire the mentality of a millionaire."

His uncle turned to a large map on the wall and pointed to a small, somewhat isolated town.

"Have you ever been there?"

"No."

"Why not give it a try? Go and find him. He just might reveal his secret to you. He lives in a fantastic house, the most beautiful one in the whole town. You shouldn't have any problem finding it."

"Why don't *you* just tell me the secret? Then I won't have to take the trouble of going there."

"Simply because I don't have the right to. When the Instant Millionaire confided it to me, the first thing he did was make me swear never to tell it to anybody. However, he did say I could refer people to him."

All of this seemed both surprising and involved to the young man. It certainly aroused his curiosity.

"Are you sure you can't tell me anything? Anything at all?"

"Absolutely positive. What I can do is recommend you highly to the Instant Millionaire."

The young man's uncle pulled out a sheet of elegant writing paper from a drawer in his massive oak desk, took his pen, and hastily scribbled a few lines. He then folded the letter, put it in an envelope, and handed it to his nephew.

"Here's your introduction," he said, "and here's the millionaire's address. One last thing. You must promise not to read this letter. If ever you *do* open it, despite my warning, and you still want it to work for you, you'll have to pretend that you haven't opened it. But how can you undo what's already been done?"

The young man didn't have the vaguest idea what his uncle was talking about, but he agreed. His uncle had always been a bit eccentric, and he was doing him a favor, after all, so he decided not to press the point. He thanked him warmly and left.

CHAPTER TWO

❧

*In which the young man
meets an elderly gardener*

T HE YOUNG MAN sped off toward the Instant
Millionaire's town, his mind racing faster than
his automobile. How hard was it going to be
to meet this man? Would he welcome an un-
announced visitor? Would he reveal his secret method
of getting rich?

Just as he approached the millionaire's house, he
was overcome by curiosity and, despite his uncle's
words of warning, opened the letter of introduction.
He was shocked. His heart rate climbed and he broke
into a sweat. He wondered whether his uncle had
made a mistake or was playing a joke on him, because
the "letter" was only a blank sheet of paper!

He was now at the gate of the millionaire's house and noticed a security guard. The guard had a stony expression; he looked as impenetrable as the enclosed fortress he was protecting.

"What can I do for you?" the guard asked drily.

"I'd like to meet the Instant Millionaire."

"Do you have an appointment?"

"No, but..."

"Well then, do you have a letter of introduction?"

The young man pulled the letter halfway out of his pocket and quickly stuffed it back in again.

"May I see your letter," the guard pressed.

The young man remembered his uncle's words, "If you open the letter, you must pretend that you haven't."

He handed the letter to the guard who "read" it. His face remained totally expressionless.

"Fine," he said, as he gave the letter back to the young man. "You may come in."

The guard showed him where to park and led him to the front door of the millionaire's luxurious, Tudor-style home. An impeccably dressed butler opened the door.

"Can I help you?" he asked.

"I want to meet the Instant Millionaire."

"He's unable to see you at the moment. Please wait for him in the garden."

The butler accompanied the young man to the entrance of a garden with a glistening pond in the middle of it. He wandered in, admiring the beautiful flowers, bushes, and trees, and then he caught sight of a gardener who was bent over a rose bush. He must have been well into his seventies or eighties, and he wore a wide-brimmed straw hat that concealed his eyes.

When the young man approached him, the gardener broke off his work and welcomed him with a smile. He had bright, cheerful blue eyes.

"What have you come here for?" he asked in a warm and friendly voice.

"I've come to meet the Instant Millionaire."

"Oh, I see. And for what reason, if you don't mind my asking?"

"Well, I . . . I'd simply like to ask him for advice. . . ."

The gardener started to go back to his roses, then he stopped and turned. "Oh, by the way, you wouldn't have ten dollars on you, would you?"

"Ten dollars?" said the young man, blushing. "It's just that... that's all I've got left on me."

"Perfect. That's all I need."

The gardener looked very dignified. His manner exuded exceptional grace and charm.

"I'd really like to give it to you," replied the young man, "but the problem is I wouldn't have any money left to get back home."

"Are you planning on going home today?"

"No-o-o... I mean, I've no idea," said the young man, now quite confused. "I don't want to leave until I've seen the Instant Millionaire."

"But if you don't need the money today, why are you so reluctant to lend it to me? You might not need it tomorrow. Who knows? You might be a millionaire."

The reasoning didn't sound completely logical to the young man, but he handed him the money. The gardener smiled.

"Most people are afraid of asking for things, and when they finally do, they don't insist enough. That's a mistake."

At that moment the butler arrived in the garden and spoke to the old man respectfully. "Sir, could you please let me have ten dollars? The cook's leaving today and insists on being paid. I'm just ten dollars short."

The gardener stuck his hand into his baggy pocket and pulled out a huge roll of bills. He must have had thousands of dollars in cash on him, because the young man caught sight of nothing but hundred-dollar bills, except for the ten-dollar bill on top. The gardener peeled off the bill he had just borrowed from the young man and handed it to the butler, who thanked him, bowed somewhat obsequiously, and quickly disappeared into the house.

The young man was outraged. How did the gardener have the gall to confiscate the last ten dollars he had in the world when his pockets were stuffed with more cash than he had ever seen?

"Why did you ask me for ten dollars?" he said, trying as hard as he could to conceal the rage he felt. "You didn't need it!"

"But of course I did. Look, I don't have any ten-dollar bills," he said, thumbing through the fat roll of cash. "You don't think I was going to give him a hundred, do you?"

"Why on earth do you keep so much money on you?"

"It's my pocket money," replied the gardener. "I always keep $25,000 on me in case of an emergency."

"Uh...$25,000?" sputtered the young man, aghast.

Suddenly everything became clear: the ever-polite butler, that incredible amount of pocket money....

"You're the Instant Millionaire, aren't you?"

"For the time being," replied the gardener. "I'm glad you've come.

"But tell me, how is it that you aren't rich yet? Have you ever seriously asked yourself that question?"

"Not really."

"Well, that's probably the first thing you should do. Think aloud in front of me, if you want. I'll try to follow your line of reasoning."

The young man made a few feeble attempts and then gave up.

"I see," said the millionaire. "You're not used to thinking out loud. Do you know there are lots of young people your age who are already rich? Some are even millionaires. Others are just on the verge of getting their first million. Did you know that when he was twenty-six, Aristotle Onassis already had

$500,000 in the bank when he left for England, where he was planning to set up his shipping empire?"

"Only twenty-six?"

"That's right. And when he started out he had only a few hundred dollars to his name. He didn't have a university degree—and he didn't have any rich uncles.

"But now it's time for dinner. Would you like to join me?"

"Thank you very much. I'd love to."

The young man followed the millionaire, who, despite his age, still had a lively bounce in his step. They went into the dining room, where the table had already been set for two.

"Please sit down." The millionaire pointed to the end of the table, the place usually reserved for the host. He sat to the right of his young guest, directly in front of a beautiful hourglass engraved with the motto *Time is Money*.

The butler arrived with a bottle of wine and filled their glasses.

"Let's drink to your first million," said the millionaire, raising his glass.

He took a sip, the only one he had all evening, and ate very modestly—just a few mouthfuls from a delicious salmon steak.

"Do you like what you do for a living?" the millionaire asked the young man.

"I suppose so. The situation in the office is a bit difficult."

"Make sure you're positive about your choice of careers. All the millionaires I've known—and I've met quite a few over the years—loved their occupations. For them, working became almost a leisure activity, as agreeable as a hobby. That's why most rich people rarely take vacations. Why should they deprive themselves of what they enjoy doing so much? And that's why they continue working even after becoming millionaires several times over.

"But though it's an absolute must to enjoy your work, it's not enough. To get rich, you have to know the secrets of wealth. Tell me, do you really believe these secrets exist?"

"Yes, I do."

"Good. That's the first step. Most people don't believe there are secrets to attaining wealth. They don't even believe they can become rich. And they're right, of course. If you don't think you can become rich, you very rarely do. You have to start by believing that you can, and then crave it passionately. Most people aren't ready to accept these secrets, even if they are revealed to them in very simple terms. Their greatest limitation is their own lack of imagination. That's why the true secrets of wealth are the best-kept secrets in the world.

"It's a little like the purloined letter in Edgar Allan Poe's story," the millionaire went on. "Do you remember it? It's the story about a letter the police were searching for and could never find, because, instead of being hidden away somewhere, it was lying in the least likely spot—in plain sight! Their lack of imagination and their built-in prejudices prevented the police from finding the letter. They weren't expecting to find it in plain sight, so they never saw it."

The young man listened to the millionaire with rapt attention. He was burning to find out what these secrets were. In any case, one thing was sure: Even if the millionaire didn't really have any secrets, he was certainly a master at setting an impressive scene.

CHAPTER THREE

*In which the young man
learns to seize opportunities
and take risks*

N OW, how much money are you willing to pay
to get these secrets of wealth?"

The millionaire's question took the young
man by surprise.

"Even if I *was* willing to spend money to get it, I
haven't got a dime."

"But *if* you had money, how much would you be
willing to pay? Name a figure, any figure. The first
one that comes to mind."

The young man couldn't possibly evade the question now. The millionaire was asking for a very specific answer.

"I don't know," he replied. "A hundred dollars...?"

The millionaire burst out laughing.

"Only a hundred dollars? Then you don't really believe these secrets exist, do you? If you did, you'd surely be ready to pay a lot more for them. Come on, I'll give you a second chance. Name another figure. This isn't a game, but a very serious matter."

The young man thought it over.

"I don't mind answering," he said. "But remember, I'm flat broke."

"Don't worry about that."

"But if I don't have any money, my hands are tied," said the young man, bewildered.

"Oh, my!" exclaimed the millionaire. "We've got a long way to go! Since time began, the rich have been using other people's money to amass their fortunes. Anyone really serious has never needed money to make money. By that I mean personal cash. Besides, you must have a checkbook on you...."

The young man wanted to deny it, but he had stuffed his checkbook into his pocket that morning. God knows why: he had exactly four dollars and twenty-eight cents in his account! He considered lying about it, but the millionaire had such a piercing gaze he seemed capable of mind-reading.

The young man heard himself stutter, as if he were confessing a deep, dark secret, "Yes, I br-brought it with me."

He pulled his checkbook out as automatically as a robot, even though an urge to rebel momentarily crossed his mind. He felt spellbound by this man, like someone in the hands of a hypnotist. Yet he wasn't afraid of the millionaire, for he radiated goodwill; he even seemed somewhat amused.

"Fine," replied the millionaire. "*Now* can you see there's no problem?"

He uncapped an elegant pen and handed it to the young man.

"Write out a check for the amount you have in mind and sign it."

"But I don't know how much to write."

"All right. Put down, say, $25,000."

The millionaire uttered this figure in a perfectly straightforward way, without a shred of arrogance.

"What ... $25,000!" exclaimed the young man. "You've got to be joking."

"Put down $50,000 if you like," replied the millionaire, so calmly that the young man no longer knew whether he spoke seriously or in jest.

"Even $25,000 seems far too much. Anyway, you couldn't cash the check because it would just bounce. And all I'd get out of it would be an angry bank manager wondering whether I'd gone crazy. And he'd be right!"

"That's exactly how I undertook my biggest deal ever. I signed a check for $250,000 and then had to scramble around to find the money to cover it. But if I hadn't made out that check right then and there, I'd have missed an excellent opportunity.

"That was one of my first major business lessons," he said. "People who waste time waiting for all the perfect conditions to fall into place never get anything done. The ideal time for action is *now*!

"Another lesson this little exercise can teach you is this: If you want to succeed in life, you have to make sure you have no choice in the matter. You have to put your back to the wall. People who vacillate and refuse to take risks because they don't have all the elements in hand never get anywhere. The reason is simple. When you cut off all your exits and put your back to the wall, you mobilize all your inner powers. You want something to happen with every fiber of your being. So why hesitate now, young man? Put your back to the wall. Make out that $25,000 check to me."

The young man wrote out the check, slowly filling in the numbers, then the words. But when he came to sign it, he simply couldn't do it.

"I've never written a check as large as this in my life."

"If you really want to become a millionaire, you'll have to start some day. You'll have to get used to signing checks much larger than this one. This is only the beginning."

But the young man still couldn't sign it. Everything was happening so quickly. He was about to hand over a check for $25,000 to a man he'd just met and who was promising some pretty dubious secrets in exchange.

"What's stopping you from signing?" asked the millionaire. "Everything's relative under the sun. In no time at all, this amount will appear insignificant to you."

"It's not the amount," mumbled the young man.

"Well, what is it, then? I know why you can't sign it. You don't really believe my secrets will turn you into a millionaire. If you were absolutely convinced, you'd sign in a flash. Tell me, if you were absolutely positive that these secrets would help you earn an additional $100,000 in less than a year, without having to work harder than you do now—even by working less—would you sign that check?"

"Sure I would," he was forced to agree. "I'd make a $75,000 profit."

"So sign it. I guarantee that you'll be able to earn that amount."

"Would you be willing to put that in writing?"

The millionaire burst out laughing once again.

"I like you, young man. You're determined to cover your back. That's often a very prudent thing to do. Even if you're absolutely sure about your resources, it doesn't mean you should trust the first person who comes your way."

He left the table, rummaged about in a drawer, and pulled out a ready-made agreement. This didn't sit very well with the young man. Was the millionaire mass-producing his secrets and selling them to every Tom, Dick, and Harry who showed up?

The millionaire signed the guarantee and handed

it to the young man, who skimmed over it quickly, satisfied with what he'd read. Then the old man suddenly changed his mind.

"I've got another idea," he said. "How about a bet?"

He took a coin from his pocket and bounced it up and down in the palm of his hand.

"Let's play heads or tails. If I lose, I'll give you the $25,000 cash I have in my pocket. If I win, you give me the check. In either case, let's forget about the guarantee."

"The only problem," the young man said, "is what I told you. There's almost nothing in my account. Even if I give you this check, you won't be able to cash it."

"No problem," said the millionaire. "I'm in no hurry. Why not postdate it a year from now?"

The young man hesitated.

"All right. Under those conditions I accept the bet."

He had now calculated that in any event he had a full year to change banks, close his account, or simply stop the check. He had nothing to lose. And with the millionaire's new offer he could even earn $25,000 in a few seconds flat, without having to do an ounce of work!

A self-satisfied smile flitted across his lips, in spite of himself. He hoped the millionaire hadn't noticed it.

The millionaire then proposed a minor clarification, which immediately confirmed the young man's doubts.

"There's just one thing. Should you lose the bet, you have to solemnly swear that you'll honor this check."

The young man tentatively gave his word, but just as the millionaire was about to toss the coin, he abruptly interrupted him.

"May I see the coin?" he asked.

The millionaire smiled.

"No doubt about it. I really like you, young man. You're cautious. That'll help you avoid a lot of mistakes. Just make sure it doesn't cause you to miss out on a lot of good opportunities."

The millionaire handed over the coin. As soon as the young man had carefully examined both sides and returned it, the millionaire asked him to call.

"Tails."

The millionaire tossed the coin, and the young man's heart began to beat as wildly as if he were on his first date! This was the first time he'd ever had the chance of winning $25,000!

As he watched the coin spinning in the air, his anxiety mounted sharply. It landed on the table.

"Heads!" said the millionaire gleefully, but then quickly added a sympathetic, "Sorry."

It was hard to say whether he was being sincere or merely polite.

The young man couldn't help trembling a little as he signed the check. He would probably get used to signing big checks like this one day, but at this point it made him feel very strange indeed.

He gave the check to the millionaire, who examined it briefly, folded it, and put it in his pocket.

"Now," said the young man, "can I have the secrets?"

"But of course," said the millionaire. "Do you have a piece of paper? I'll write them down for you. That way, you won't forget them."

The young man had a hard time grasping his words. The millionaire surely couldn't expect a single sheet of paper to hold all the secrets—especially secrets he'd just bought for $25,000!

"Sorry. I don't have any paper on me."

"But didn't you have a letter of introduction when you arrived here? The people your uncle has sent me over the years always had a letter."

The young man took it out of his pocket.

He handed it over, carefully watching the old man's face as he opened it. But the millionaire didn't seem at all surprised to find it was completely blank. He took his pen, leaned over the table, and was about to write something when he raised his head and asked the young man to fetch the butler.

"You'll find him in the kitchen, at the far end of that corridor over there," explained the millionaire.

When the young man came back with the butler, the millionaire was sealing the envelope. He seemed pleased with himself.

"Our young guest will be spending the night," he said to the butler. "Would you take him to his room, please?"

Then he turned to the young man and said, "Here are the secrets." He stood up and handed him the envelope; then he solemnly shook his hand, as if he had just wrapped up one of the most important deals he had ever made in his life.

"The only thing I must ask you to do is to wait until you're alone in your room before opening the envelope and reading the secrets. And oh, there's one more condition. Before you may read what I've written, you must promise to spend part of your life sharing these secrets with those less fortunate than you. If you agree, you'll be the last person to whom I'll ever give these secrets directly. My work here will be over. I'll be ready to take care of roses in a much larger garden.

"If you don't feel ready to share these secrets," he said, "you still have time to back out. But then, of course, you won't be able to open the envelope. I'll give you back your check. And you'll be free to go home and get on with the same life you've been leading up to now."

Now that he finally had his hands on the letter containing the secrets, there was no possibility of backing out. His curiosity had gotten the better of him.

"I promise," he replied.

CHAPTER FOUR

*In which the young man
finds himself a prisoner*

SOON THE YOUNG MAN was alone in his room, a room so luxurious he couldn't help examining it. He went up to the only window, which was very high off the ground, and looked out over the park. He could see where he had first spotted the millionaire looking after his roses with such tender, loving care.

Night had fallen, and a full moon cast a luminescent glow over everything. He was filled with anticipation. He was finally going to discover the secrets to making the fortune that had eluded him for so many years.

He slowly opened the envelope and unfolded the

letter. The sheet of paper was again completely blank! He turned it over. There wasn't the tiniest squiggle on either side. He'd been fool enough to let the old man swindle him! He'd handed over a check for a mind-boggling sum in exchange for something that didn't exist!

The millionaire had seemed so honest. He'd even started feeling fond of the old man.

The young man realized that he should have been more careful, that perhaps there was some truth after all in the belief that totally honest people never get rich. He was forced to admit that he had no business sense at all—probably the very reason he was still poor. And now even poorer! A feeling of rebellion engulfed him and he threw the paper across the room.

What could he do? He'd let himself be lured into a well-sprung trap. He had only one alternative: to leave as quickly as possible. Who knows? Maybe his life was in danger, too. He didn't want to spend the night in this place.

He decided the best thing to do would be to sneak out as quietly as possible. He tiptoed to the door and slowly turned the handle, but the door was bolted from the outside. The window was the only other exit, and it was about thirty feet above the ground. If he jumped, he'd surely break his neck. His only option was to ring for the butler.

He pulled the bell and waited. No one came.

He rang again. Nothing. Maybe the bell was out of order.

The house was totally silent. He was a prisoner.

He lay on the bed and the events of the day raced before his eyes. There was little he could do to fight off the feeling of absurdity that was beginning to overwhelm him. The blank sheet of paper he had bought for $25,000 kept drifting before him, as if bent on mocking him.

Sleep finally overtook him. He dreamed of a stranger luring him repeatedly to sign a thick document of the utmost importance, as if his life depended on it. He protested vehemently. There must be some mistake—the document is totally blank....

CHAPTER FIVE

◆✦◆

*In which the young man
learns to have faith*

THE NEXT MORNING the young man felt as
if he'd been run over by a three-ton truck.

He glanced at himself in the mirror. He
had slept in his clothes and looked awful but
it only bolstered his determination. He had one thought
in mind: to find the old man, give him back his
"secret," and get his check back.

He ran his fingers through his hair and headed
toward the door, recalling it had been locked the
night before. It wasn't now. He strode out angrily and
headed for the dining room.

He found the millionaire sitting calmly at the table,
dressed in the same clothes he'd had on the day

before: clean but surprisingly threadbare gardener's clothes. His large, pointed, wide-brimmed hat was lying in front of him on the table.

The millionaire was flipping a coin in the air and counting as it landed on the table.

"Nine," he muttered without taking his eyes off the coin.

"Ten...damn!" He lifted his head.

"I've never been able to go beyond ten," he said. "I get what I want ten times in a row and then invariably it fails on the eleventh throw, even though I toss it exactly the same way each time."

The young man realized he had been duped the night before.

"My father, who was an accomplished magician, would regularly get to fifteen," said the millionaire. "I didn't inherit his talent."

The young man asked to see the coin. The millionaire cheerfully gave it to him, and the young man flipped it onto the table. Heads. Tails. Heads. Tails. It obviously wasn't a trick coin, unless there was some secret mechanism that escaped his notice.

"There was nothing dishonest about our bet yesterday," said the millionaire. "I simply displayed my skill at handling money. Some people take skillfulness for dishonesty, but they're two very different things."

The young man brandished the letter and threw it on the table.

"You did a fine job of tricking me, sir. You made yourself some easy money there: $25,000 for a blank sheet of paper."

"It's the secret of wealth," the millionaire said.

"Well, you're going to have to explain yourself. Do you take me for an idiot?"

"An idiot? Of course not. You're simply lacking in insight. It's quite normal. Your mind is still immature."

"Maybe it is, but I can certainly recognize a blank piece of paper when I see one."

"I assure you that you can become very rich indeed with just this blank piece of paper. That's all I needed to become an instant millionaire way back when. But since I must soon go back to tend my beloved roses, I'll help you. Listen carefully, because as soon as you apply this secret successfully, you'll have to share it with others. Once you've freed yourself of the shackles of poverty, you'll have to show the way to those still bound hand and foot. May I ask you to repeat the promise you made yesterday?"

There was no doubt about it; the millionaire was an extraordinarily persuasive man. Just a few minutes before the young man had been ready to curse him and now he was listening attentively.

He repeated his promise.

"I must warn you that becoming a millionaire will probably seem too easy. But don't let simplicity deceive you. Each time you begin to have doubts, remember Mozart: true genius resides in simplicity. You'll tend to have doubts in the beginning. With time, as wealth is magnetically attracted to you in a most unexpected way, you'll begin to understand."

"That's exactly what I've been hoping for with all my heart: to understand!"

"So much the better. Once you've grasped this secret, you'll know why you believe in it. But in the beginning, despite its simplicity, this secret will seem so surprising that you'll be incapable of understanding it—or even believing it, for that matter. So I have to ask you to make a small leap of faith. If the secret exists, you'll have gained everything because of your faith. If it doesn't, you won't have lost a thing."

CHAPTER SIX

*In which the young man
learns to focus on a goal*

F EEL FREE to ask me any questions that cross
your mind," said the millionaire. "It'll be a
pleasure for me to answer them. Soon you
won't be able to do so. Our time together is
limited, so let's not waste it in futile discussions.
Here's a pen. Do you have the piece of paper?"

"Here it is."

"Do you really want to become rich?"

"I most certainly do."

"All right, then. Write down the amount of money
you want and how much time you'll allow yourself to
acquire it."

"Do you think money's going to drop like pennies

from heaven just because I write a couple of numbers down on paper?"

"Yes, I do," said the millionaire. "I warned you that the secret would be simple. All the millionaires I've met told me they became rich the moment they set themselves an amount and a deadline by which to acquire it. If you don't know where you're heading, the chances are you'll never get anywhere."

"It sounds like magic to me."

"But that's exactly what it is—the magic of a *quantified objective.*

"Let's look at the problem from a different angle. Suppose you're trying to get a job. You go through all the necessary steps and finally get an interview. A short while later, you're told that you're being seriously considered. Then you find out you've got the job and that you'll be making a lot of money. How would you react? For a start, you'd be really pleased with yourself. Being chosen from dozens, perhaps hundreds of candidates—what a feat! And since you were unemployed for, say, three months, you'd think this was a very lucky break indeed. But once your initial euphoria had passed, what would be your next reaction?"

"Well, I'd wonder when the job would start. Then, I'd like to know the exact meaning of 'a lot of money.' All things being relative, I'd try and find out exactly how much the salary was going to be and what kind of benefits would be offered."

"Good! If, for example, you asked your new boss what he meant by 'a lot of money' and all he was willing to do was guarantee that you would definitely earn a lot, you wouldn't be satisfied, would you? Worse yet, you'd probably start having second thoughts about his honesty. The fact that he refused to name a specific figure could quite possibly mean that there was something shady going on, and that your salary wasn't going to be as generous as he'd been implying. And if he refused to tell you the exact date you were supposed to start the job, you would really be suspicious, wouldn't you? You'd try to pin him down."

"I suppose I would," agreed the young man.

"And if you insisted on it and still couldn't get the details you wanted, you might just turn it down and start looking elsewhere. In fact, you'd be fully justified in doing so."

"You're right. The offer leaves a lot to be desired."

The millionaire looked content. He paused a moment before proceeding, his lips still set in a teasing but good-natured smile.

"The questions you asked your potential employer were aimed at getting hard facts. Right? Just knowing that you were going to earn a lot of money wasn't enough. You also wanted to know how much. Finding out that you'd been given the job didn't satisfy you, either. You also wanted to know the exact starting date. And you'd probably want all of this in writing, because a contract adds backbone to a verbal agreement. Spoken words are ephemeral but the written word is permanent.

"What most people, or at least the unsuccessful ones, are unaware of is that life gives us exactly what we ask from it. The first thing to do, therefore, is to ask for exactly what you want. If your request is vague, whatever you get will be just as muddled. If you ask for the minimum, you'll get the minimum.

"Any request you make must be absolutely precise. As far as monetary wealth is concerned, you must establish an amount and a deadline by which to make it. What do people generally do? Even those who want money and lots of it all make the same mistake: they don't establish an exact amount and a deadline by which to make it. If you need convincing, just ask someone exactly how much money he wants to earn next year. Ask him to reply right away. If this person is really on the road to success, if he really knows where he's going, and if he doesn't mind confiding in you, he'll be able to answer immediately. Nine out of ten people, however, will be incapable of answering this simple question off the top of their heads. It is the most common mistake. Life wants to know exactly what you expect from it. If you don't ask for anything, you won't get anything.

"Now let's test you," the old man said. "You told me you'd like to get rich."

"Definitely."

"Tell me how much you'd like to earn next year."

The young man found himself at a loss for words. He had had no trouble following the old man's line of reasoning. In fact, he had agreed with it wholeheartedly. And yet he had to admit that he belonged to the vast majority of people who want to get rich but don't know how much they want to make. He was embarrassed.

"I don't know," he was forced to admit. "But I think I've just understood one of my mistakes— perhaps the most fundamental one."

"It is a serious mistake. Let's try to correct it. Come on, write down the amount you have in mind."

"I really don't have the vaguest idea," muttered the young man.

"And yet it's so easy. Write down the amount you'd like to earn in the next year. I know what we'll do. Take a few minutes to think it over. When the time's up, you've *got* to write down an amount. We've already established the deadline: one year from today. So all you have to think about is the amount. Get going! Time's slipping away!"

As he said this, he picked up the golden hourglass on the table and turned it over.

The young man quickly got into the spirit of the game, and realized it was the first time he'd had to concentrate so hard in his life. All sorts of numbers flitted about uncontrollably in his head. Time was running out. When the last grain of sand had fallen, he still hadn't settled on a specific figure.

"Good," said the millionaire, who hadn't taken his

eyes away from the hourglass. "What figure do you have in mind?"

The young man finally picked the most expansive figure he thought he was capable of making, and slowly wrote down the numbers.

"Only $50,000!" exclaimed the millionaire. "That's pretty low—but it's a start. I would have preferred $500,000. You've got quite a lot of work to do before becoming an instant millionaire. But you'll see; it won't be as tiring as most people imagine it to be. And it'll be the most important work you'll ever do in your life, no matter what occupation you end up choosing. It's called working on *yourself*."

CHAPTER SEVEN

❧

*In which the young man
gets to know the
value of self-image*

T HE BUTLER came into the dining room carrying coffee and croissants, and the young man ate while the lesson continued.

"I'm going to ask you a series of questions," said the millionaire, "to help you understand what happened to you during your few minutes of reflection.

"The first thing you must realize is that the amount you wrote down on that piece of paper means much more than you think it does. In fact, that amount represents almost to a penny what you think you're worth. In your eyes, whether you are willing to admit it or not, you're worth $50,000 a year. Not a penny more and not a penny less."

"I don't see how you can say that," said the young man. "The fact that I chose that particular amount means I'm level-headed and have both feet on the ground. I just can't see how I can earn more for the time being. After all, I don't have a very well-paying job, or a degree, or anything in the bank."

"Your way of thinking is valid to an extent. In any case, I respect it. The only problem is, this attitude is the cause of your current situation. External circumstances are not really very important. Keep this well in mind: *All the events in your life are a mirror image of your thoughts*. Your mind can't grasp this principle if you continue to accept the widespread illusion that external factors determine your life. In reality, everything in life is a matter of attitude. Life is exactly as you picture it. Everything that happens to you is a product of your thoughts. So if you want to change your life, you must start by changing your thoughts. No doubt you consider this a bit trite. Many 'rational' individuals stubbornly refute this principle.

"But the truth is, all those who have accomplished great things in life, regardless of the field, have always ignored the objections raised by strictly 'rational' thinkers.

"This certainly doesn't mean I'm against intelligence in any way. Quite the contrary. Reasoning and logic are essential in order to achieve success. But they aren't enough. They must be instruments and faithful servants, nothing more.

"In most cases reasoning and logic become roadblocks in the way of great achievement, because great things are created only by those who have faith in the powers of the mind. Successful people never let circumstances bother them too much. When you come down to it, the circumstances facing great achievers in the past were just as difficult—and often even more difficult—than those facing their contemporaries, but this simply caused them to reach even deeper to tap their inner strength. Those achievers firmly believed that they could accomplish great things. All those who became rich were deeply convinced that they could get rich. And that's why they succeeded.

"But let's get back to our piece of paper and answer this question: The $50,000 figure you wrote down was surely not the largest one that came to your mind, was it?"

"You're right. It wasn't."

"What was, then?"

"My head was crowded with so many numbers...."

"For instance?"

"Well, $100,000."

"And why didn't you write it down?"

"I don't know. I suppose it seemed totally out of reach."

"It'll remain that way until you believe you can reach it.

"Since you started with only $50,000, we've got a big job ahead of us; and if we don't do it, it'll take you a very long time to become a millionaire. So write down the highest figure that now seems achievable to you. Stretch yourself."

After a moment of reflection, the young man wrote down $75,000.

"Congratulations," the millionaire responded quickly. "You've just earned $25,000 in a few seconds. Not bad, eh?"

"I haven't earned it yet."

"It's as if you had. You've taken the biggest step. You expanded your self-image by considering you could earn $75,000 instead of $50,000. It's not a major leap forward, but it's progress all the same. Rome wasn't built in a day, after all.

"Inside you lies a kind of Rome—as it does in every human being. The astonishing thing is that this city is both exactly as you picture it, and it's also surprisingly flexible. The size of your city depends on the exact circumference you give it. By increasing the figure you wrote down, you expanded your city limits. Your inner Rome grew, and it's just a beginning.

"All wise thinkers have said for ages that the greatest limitations are those man imposes on himself, and thus the greatest obstacle to success is a mental obstacle. Expand your mental limits and you will expand the limits of your life. Explode your limitations and you will explode the limitations of your life. The conditions in your life will change as if by magic. I swear by experience this is true."

"But how can I find out what my mental limitations are?" the young man asked. "All this seems plausible, yet at the same time quite abstract."

"I've just explained how to find the boundary that corresponds to your self-image," said the millionaire. "You translated it into concrete terms when you wrote down that number. It's fascinating to see what each individual really thinks of himself. Each time someone does this exercise, a single figure immediately exposes his true self-image. He is confronted by his mental limitations, which will perfectly match the limits he encounters in life. Life will bow before the limits he sets for himself—whether he is aware of this or not. People who generally fail are the least conscious of these key principles of success and wealth. Successful individuals have become aware of this phenomenon and have done their utmost to work on their self-image.

"The easiest way to work on this self-image in the beginning is to take a blank sheet of paper and write down steadily increasing amounts. Let's start our little exercise over again. Write down a much bolder figure this time."

The young man thought for a few seconds and, squirming, wrote down $100,000, confessing that this was the maximum he could imagine earning.

"Maybe it's the maximum you can imagine, but it's definitely not the maximum you could *actually* earn. That's a pretty modest figure. Some people earn it in a month, others in a week, even a day—

every day of the year. However, let me congratulate you. You've made astounding progress: you've doubled your earnings and considerably extended your mental boundaries—not as much as I would like, but I don't want to rush you. You have to start by setting yourself an objective that you consider bold but at the same time reasonable.

"The secret of any goal is that it must be both ambitious *and* within reach. But don't forget that most people are overly conservative—they're afraid to burst through their mental limitations. They've turned their mental limitations into a kind of habit. They're used to going without. They're convinced that's what life's all about. They're scared to dream.

"You mustn't be afraid of expanding your mental boundaries. What you can accomplish in an hour, merely by writing down a series of larger and larger numbers, is amazing. You've managed to double your goal within a matter of a few minutes. Later on, when you're alone, do the next exercise. Sit down in the privacy of your own room and write out the course of your financial destiny. This is how to do it. Write: *In six years to the day I will be a millionaire.* This is the practical application of my secret to becoming an instant millionaire. You'll probably object to the fact that it'll take you six long years to become a millionaire. I agree, but it'll take you only a second to activate the secret key that will ensure your financial destiny and fortune.

"As for me, I started out with some cash that an old millionaire lent me—equivalent to about $25,000 in today's dollars—and it took me precisely five years and nine months to make my first million. Ever since then, I've made it prosper by using the same formula over and over, with ever-increasing numbers. This formula has always made some people laugh, and that's not going to change. However, the ones who laugh aren't rich!"

The young man shook his head pensively. He was half convinced. But it all seemed a bit too easy.

"Obviously," continued the millionaire, "this formula is effective for those who want to become something other than millionaires. After all, not everyone cherishes that ambition. And that's precisely the beauty of this secret. It works equally well for any dream— from the most modest to the most extravagant. It can make you an extra $5,000 a year or double your income in a year—something that's totally feasible, by the way.

"So, if you don't mind, go and spend some time in your room while I go back to my precious roses, and write the sentence I gave you: *In six years to the day, I will be a millionaire. I will therefore be a millionaire on*, and then write the month, the day, and the year. Make sure you take note of every impression that comes into your mind, no matter what it may be. You'll find some paper in the desk. Remember one thing: As long as you aren't used to the idea of becoming a millionaire, as long as it isn't an integral part of your life and thus of your innermost thoughts, nothing can help you become a millionaire.

"Go now and reflect on my formula or affirmation, as you may wish to call it. Let it become your guiding principle during the next six years."

CHAPTER EIGHT

~✦~

*In which the young man
discovers the power of words*

A N HOUR LATER the butler came to fetch the
young man, who had been so engrossed in the
exercise the eccentric millionaire had given
him to do, that it seemed as if no time at all
had passed.

The butler explained that the millionaire was expecting him in the garden, and he accompanied the
young man there in silence. His host was sitting on a
bench, contemplating a freshly cut rose. He raised
his head when he heard the young man approach. A
gentle smile lit his face; he was radiant, in fact, he
seemed almost ecstatic.

"So, how did it go?" he asked. "Did the exercise work out all right?"

"Yes, it did. But I've got a lot of questions."

"That's what I'm here for."

He invited the young man to sit next to him.

"What bothers me in particular," he told the old man, "is that I just can't see how I can become a millionaire in six years even if I do write down this crazy sentence and meditate on it. How can I *convince* myself that I can become a millionaire? I don't even know which field I want to work in. And I still feel I'm pretty young to become a millionaire."

"Youth is no obstacle. Countless people became rich at a much younger age than yours. The major obstacle is not knowing the secret, or knowing it and not applying it."

"I feel ready to apply it. But the only trouble is that I don't think I can *honestly* convince myself that I can become a millionaire."

"There's basically only one way to do it. And it's the same method you use to persuade yourself that you *can't* become a millionaire even if you want to.

"During the next few days, or few weeks at the

most, you are going to develop the attitude of an instant millionaire. Naturally, it's going to take some time to undo everything you've built up over the years.

"The secret to developing this personality resides in words, combined with images, which are the special way in which thoughts express themselves. Each thought you have tends to manifest itself in your life in one way or another. The stronger a person's character is, the more powerful his thoughts will be, and the more quickly they will tend to manifest, thus shaping the circumstances of his life. This undoubtedly inspired the early Greek philosopher Heraclitus to observe, 'Character equals destiny.'

"Desire is what best sustains your thoughts. The more passionate your desire is, the more quickly the thing you want will spring up in your life. The way to become rich is to desire it fervently. In every area of life, sincerity and fervor are necessary ingredients of success."

"And yet I sincerely wish to be rich," said the young man. "I've been doing everything possible for years now. But nothing's worked out."

"Ardent desire is necessary, but not enough. What you lack is faith. You must *believe* that you will become a millionaire."

"How can I get this faith?"

"I've read a great many books on this subject. And what my own mentor taught me corresponds to the conclusions reached in them: *The way to obtain faith is through the repetition of words.* Words have an extraordinary impact on our inner and outer lives. Words are omnipotent. Most people are totally unaware of this principle and fail to use it—no, I take that back. They do use the power of words, but generally to their detriment."

"I don't want to contradict you," said the young man, "but I think you're exaggerating. I can't really see how words can help me become a millionaire. They have some importance, but certainly other things are more important, and more powerful."

The millionaire didn't respond. He was absorbed in his own thoughts for a moment. Then he said, "In the desk up in your room I left a booklet that explains this theory in a very enlightening way. Go and find it. It's very short. Read it and come down again. We'll continue our discussion then."

The young man went back to his room, closed the door and searched for the booklet in the desk. There was no booklet, but he found a letter that was apparently addressed to him even though it didn't have his name written on it. It was inscribed, *Letter to a Young Millionaire.*

He opened it. It contained a single word written in red ink: FAREWELL. It was signed, *The Instant Millionaire.*

The young man's heart began to flutter like a butterfly gone mad. At that moment he heard a strange sound behind him. He turned around and saw a computer he had not previously noticed. The printer was spitting out some words extremely fast. The young man approached it and began to read the printout. It contained one sentence repeated over and over again:

YOU HAVE AN HOUR LEFT TO LIVE.

YOU HAVE AN HOUR LEFT TO LIVE.

YOU HAVE AN HOUR LEFT TO LIVE.

YOU HAVE AN HOUR LEFT TO LIVE.

If this was a joke, it was certainly in bad taste. It had to be a joke, though. Why would the Instant Millionaire want him to die? The young man hadn't done anything to him. But everything was so strange in this place. Maybe the millionaire was a madman hiding his murderous tendencies behind a veneer of kindheartedness.

The young man was terribly confused. He was sure of one thing, however: whether or not this was a joke, he wasn't going to take any risks. He was going to make his escape, and forget about his check and the magical theories the millionaire had used to fuel his gullible imagination.

He threw the letter on the floor and made for the door, but again it was firmly locked. He was overwhelmed with panic. He shook the handle, trying to force the door open, but it was hopeless.

The young man went wild. He ran to the window and saw the millionaire working in the garden. He shouted to him. No answer. He screamed more frantically. Again no answer. The butler stepped into the garden, and the young man called out to him in an hysterical voice. But it was as if his shouts didn't exist.

What kind of horrible nightmare was he going through?

He called again and again. Another servant appeared a few paces behind the butler. He, too, was

completely oblivious to the prisoner's screams for help.
The young man became more and more desperate.

As he spun around helplessly, he spotted a telephone. What an idiot he was! Why hadn't he thought
of that last time? Perhaps, like the computer, it hadn't
been there.

He called the operator and asked for the nearest
police station. She gave him a number...she had a
most unusual voice. He called quickly, but got a busy
signal. What an exasperating sound! He called again.
Still busy. He tried again and again and again—then
noticed that the number he was calling was right
before his eyes. It was the one on the telephone he
was using. He was calling his own room!

He frantically searched for something with which
to pry open the door. As he passed the window, he
noticed a man approaching the house. He was wear-
ing an immense black cloak and a wide-brimmed
black hat. The young man's chest was constricted;
he was almost suffocating with terror. Who could it
be but a hired assassin coming to get him? It was
clear. He was trapped. He was going to die.

Soon he heard heavy footsteps slowly making their
way toward the door. He was right. His time had

finally come. He searched left and right for something, anything, with which to defend himself, but could find nothing. He heard the key turning in the lock. The handle moved, the door opened.

Standing in the doorway was a murky black shadow, which swiftly turned into the more substantial figure of a man, standing silently, motionless as a statue. Then the man plunged his hand into his pocket. The young man thought he was going to pull out a weapon, but the mysterious stranger drew out a piece of paper instead. He lifted the brim of his hat and the young man, breathlessly expecting the worst, saw it was the millionaire.

"You forgot the figures you came up with in the garden," said the millionaire. "Did you find the booklet I told you about?"

"No, I didn't. I found this instead," the young man said angrily.

He retrieved the letter from the floor.

"What's the meaning of this grotesque scenario you just played out?" demanded the young man. "I could sue you, you know...."

"But... they're only words, a word scribbled on a piece of paper, a few words on a computer screen.

Didn't you tell me that you didn't believe in the power of words? Look at the state you're in...."

The young man suddenly realized what the millionaire was talking about.

"I just wanted to give you a quick lesson. Experience is a much better teacher than mere theory. Experience is life. Wasn't that Goethe's philosophy? Gray is the color of theory; green, the color of the tree of life.

"Now do you understand the power that words have? Their power is so great they don't even need to be true to have an effect on people. I assure you I did not at any time have criminal intentions toward you."

"How was I to know that?" said the young man, gradually calming down.

"You could have used your head and reasoned things out. Why on earth would I want to kill you? You've never done me any harm. Even if you had, I would never waste time on revenge. All I want is to be free to tend my rose garden.

"You should have relied on your sense of logic. Yet, did you notice how powerless logic is in a situation such as this? When you were shouting to us from the window and we were pretending not to hear, you wer‑

truly in despair. The mistake you made wasn't in reading the words, but in believing them. By doing so you instinctively obeyed one of the greatest laws governing the human mind: When imagination and logic are in conflict with each other, the imagination invariably takes over."

The millionaire then went up to the printer, tore out the sheet, and handed it to the young man. "You lost your head over a threat that wasn't even directed at you."

At the top of the page a stranger's name was written. The young man was aghast; not only was the warning sheer fabrication, but it wasn't intended for him in the first place.

CHAPTER NINE

❦

In which the young man
is first shown the
heart of the rose

Y OU'VE LEARNED many important things today," the millionaire told the young man. "Anc
hopefully you've understood them not only with
your head but with your heart as well.

"Now you know that words deeply affect our lives
whether we wish them to or not. A thought, even
when false, can affect us if we believe it to be true.
When you learn to distinguish the value of a thought,
that is, the value you give it, your mind can regain or
maintain its calm. It was your mind that gave meaning to the threat. If it had been written in a foreign
language, you wouldn't have paid the slightest attention to it."

The millionaire was silent for a moment, then continued.

"In the future, each time you come face to face with a problem—and the road to fortune is strewn with obstacles—remember this particular threat. Remind yourself that the problem facing you has as little to do with you as this threat did. This might seem unrealistic to you, since you're the one who has to deal with the problem. But you don't have to shoulder the anxiety it breeds, or let a problem acquire so much importance that it traumatizes you. By the time you have reached this point—and it's not easy, I assure you—you will have mastered an invaluable skill and will be able to fulfill all your dreams.

"Let me warn you, however. The journey may be long and arduous before you manage to master it. But never give up. I promise you, it'll be worth your while. One day you will learn that mastering your destiny and fulfilling your dreams is the ultimate purpose of life. The rest is unimportant."

They both remained silent, absorbed in their thoughts. The young man noticed the millionaire's eyes filling with sadness....

The millionaire continued, as if summing up

everything he had said up to that point: "Life can be a rose garden or hell on earth, depending on your frame of mind. Think of the rose often. Lose yourself in the heart of a rose each time a problem crops up. And remember, you don't have to shoulder the burden of your problems."

He placed particular emphasis on the following words: "Most people cannot understand what I've just said. They believe it to be pure, unadulterated optimism. But it's much more profound than that. The world is but a reflection of your inner self. The conditions in your life are but a mirror image of your inner life. Concentrate on the heart of the rose and there you will find truth and the intuition you will need to guide you through life.

"You will also find the dual secret of true wealth: love for whatever you do, and love for others."

CHAPTER TEN

*In which the young man
learns to master
his unconscious mind*

A FTER THIS LONG and heartfelt statement the old millionaire seemed exhausted, and became silent for several minutes. Then he continued, carefully stressing each word.

"The formula, or affirmation, I have given you is so powerful. Even if in the beginning you believe it highly unlikely you will ever become a millionaire, you *will* be able to become one. Just do the same thing with the formula that you did with the message on the computer—accept it as the truth. If you have faith that you will be able to accomplish something, you will."

"In the case of the computer," the young man said,

"I let myself be tricked. I lost my head. But this formula is a different matter altogether—I have a problem believing I can become a millionaire six years from now."

"Even if you don't believe in the formula now, it'll begin acting on you. The more you internalize it, the more powerful it becomes. It's not your reasoning or *conscious* mind that you must convince. Remember the threat. Part of you—your imagination—accepted it as real. And the imagination is what some people call the *unconscious* mind. It is the hidden part of your mind, and much more powerful than the conscious part. It guides your entire life. I could spend hours talking to you about the theory of the unconscious. But it's enough for you to know that the unconscious is extremely susceptible to the power of words. Now do you know why you are having so much difficulty believing the undeniable fact that you can become a millionaire in less than six years?"

"Sorry. I don't."

"Well, the fact remains that for years and years you've been telling yourself you can't. Words have been engraving themselves in your unconscious. Deeply. In fact every experience, every thought you've ever had, every word you've ever heard has become indelibly etched in your unconscious. In the long run, this prodigious memory becomes your self-image. Without realizing it, your past experiences and your inner monologue have convinced you that you aren't the type of person who can become a millionaire, even if, objectively speaking, you have all the qualities to do so, and you could do so, more easily than you can imagine. Like everyone else, your self-image is so powerful that it unwittingly becomes your destiny. Outer circumstances end up matching the image you have of yourself with amazing precision. To become rich, you have to create a new self-image."

"Perhaps I can. I'm quite willing to try. The only snag is that I'm not really sure where to start."

"Think about the threat you experienced. It wasn't real, yet it affected you as if it was. All you have to do is play the same trick on yourself. Your unconscious won't be any the wiser for it. From the time you were a child, each suggestion you accepted, even though it was false, in effect tricked your unconscious. You may have accepted something that was patently untrue. So now you're going to experience the same thing. Your unconscious can be influenced at will; it is as easy as child's play. And once it has been influenced in the way you want it to be, you will be able to obtain exactly what you want out of life. Why? Because your unconscious will be convinced that you *can* obtain all these things. It will accept them as true in the same way that it's now accepting the fact that you can't get more out of life. This ties in with what I said earlier. Man is the reflection of the thoughts stored in his unconscious.

"The most important thing is to pretend, as best you can, that something is true. Why does this work with the unconscious? Simply because, though the unconscious may be powerful, it cannot discriminate between truth and falsehood."

"Yes, but what happens if there's a conflict between my conscious and unconscious? What happens if my conscious mind refuses to accept the idea of wealth?"

"The best solution is *repetition*. This technique is commonly called self-suggestion. Each one of us is subject to it throughout our lives. Every day we are influenced by inner and outer suggestions. The inner monologue that all of us live with continually shapes our lives. Some of us repeat to ourselves that we will never be successful because we come from a family of losers, or because we have had failures, or because we think we haven't had enough education, or don't have enough money, or skills, or intelligence, or management ability, or good luck; and on and on it goes. So we drift from failure to failure, not because we don't have the necessary qualities to succeed, but because that's how we unconsciously picture ourselves.

"Some people believe they will never attract a partner," the millionaire continued. "And yet they have all kinds of attractive qualities. Potential partners run from them like the plague. The power of their self-image, which is the reflection of the unconscious, is responsible for this. It brings about the circumstances that make others avoid them.

"But the repetition of negative formulas, which have such a tremendous impact on our lives, can be used in a different way. And that's what we're going to do. The unconscious is a slave that can dominate us because it is immensely powerful. But it is also blind, and you have to learn how to play tricks on it."

The young man didn't fully understand everything the millionaire was saying, yet he was eager to find out more.

"The beauty of this theory is that you don't really have to believe in it to use it," the millionaire said. "But to get results you have to put it to use: they won't come magically on their own. Everything, as I've said, depends on repetition. Even if you don't believe it at first, try it—at least for a couple of days. That's long enough for you to start feeling its effects.

"This might seem simplistic, but let me tell you it is the most potent secret on the face of the earth. Words have tremendous power. Remember the first words of St. John in the Bible: 'In the beginning was the Word.' Self-suggestion plays a major role in our lives. If you remain unaware of it, it will work against you more often than not. But if you decide to use it, all its tremendous power will be at your disposal."

"Well, I think you've convinced me to try," said the young man, "although, to tell you the truth, I'm still a little suspicious."

"That's all right. Just remember to base your judgment on the results, rather than on intellectual criteria. Now, come with me and I'll show you what to do."

CHAPTER ELEVEN

～

*In which the young man
and his mentor discuss
figures and formulas*

T HE MILLIONAIRE sat down at the desk and
invited the young man to join him. He took
out some paper and a pen and wrote some
figures.

"Your formula could look like this," he said. What
he had written was, *By the end of this year I will possess
assets worth $31,250. I will double those assets every year
for five years, so that by* (and here he left a space) *I will
be a millionaire.*

"You mustn't confuse assets and income," he told
the young man. "Your assets are whatever you have
left over after your current bills and taxes are paid.
Assets can comprise real estate investments, stocks

or bonds, savings in banks or mutual funds, gold, art, jewelry, valuable collectibles, and so on. Now if you want to be a millionaire in six years—which is the realistic objective I'm proposing—your formula will have to be set up on this model. If you have assets worth $31,250 by the end of the first year, you will have to double them each year. And in six years you will be a millionaire!

"Why double your assets each year? *Because it's a simple operation that your subconscious can easily handle.* And it's easy for you to remember. It also guarantees you constant growth.

"If this starting point seems too ambitious for you, then give yourself another year. Becoming a millionaire in seven years is still pretty good! Your goal for the first year will then be to have assets of $15,625. Believe me when I tell you it's far from being beyond reach. If you're convinced that you can have a cozy nest egg worth $15,625 by the end of the first year, you *will* have it.

"Now if that still seems over-ambitious, give yourself yet another year, making a total of eight. Then the goal for your first year will be $7,812.50.

"Along with your formula and the affirmation *I will*

be a millionaire on (put the month and year, in six, seven, or eight years' time), you will also have to set yourself short-term objectives, landmarks to help motivate you during your journey on the road to riches. And an annual goal is essential.

"The most important thing, however," he told his pupil, "is to write your goals down on paper. Take a pencil and fool around with figures and years. Don't be afraid; it can't do you any harm. The amounts will become more and more familiar to you as you play around with them. Millions of people want to get rich, and yet not one out of a hundred takes the initiative to outline the route he intends to take to reach his goal. Be different! Set up your plans and charts. Work out projections until you've found the plan that suits you. It'll be *your* plan.

"Use the examples I've provided for inspiration, but then let your imagination run wild. You have to start by dreaming to get rich. Then you have to know how to quantify your dream and translate it into specific sums of money and dates. This, in fact, should be the first exercise you do. Juggle numbers. You will soon see that this little game will reveal who you really are.

"The simple act of putting your goals, deadlines, and sums on paper is the first step toward transforming your ideal into its material equivalent.

"Anyone who wants to stick to an ambition of becoming a millionaire in five or ten years must take note of this fact: If he is currently earning $20,000 a year and can expect nothing more than, say, an annual ten percent raise, and if he can save and invest only a small percentage of that, then he'll never become a millionaire if he remains in his job without sideline activities.

"There's nothing reprehensible in this; it's purely an objective observation. The formula of doubling your fortune each year or increasing your assets with respect to the previous years' is clearly not the only way to become a millionaire. However, the secret it contains, that is, a quantified goal (an amount and a deadline by which to reach it), is valid for anyone wishing to succeed in any way.

"For example, you might simply want to increase your income by $5,000 a year. If you now earn $25,000, you would probably like to earn $30,000—a matter of affording a few more luxuries. Or perhaps you are earning $30,000 and would like $40,000 to enable you to trade up from your present house without worrying about the extra mortgage payments. Or you might want to be able to afford a new car, one that is a little more luxurious.

"To do this, simply repeat to yourself: *This year I will increase my income by $5,000 or $10,000 and I will earn $30,000 or $40,000* (as the case may be).

"You don't need to know how you'll manage it. You simply have to realize that if all you can hope for is a ten percent annual pay raise in your present job, and you don't want to moonlight, you will have to land a promotion or switch jobs to reach your goal. This may appear self-evident, but thousands of people hope to improve their material situation and do absolutely nothing about it. Is this ignorance? Is it because they are basically satisfied with their situations even though they complain day in and day out?

"Once you've discovered that you need some kind of change in your life to reach your goals, you might find yourself thinking that you have no other possibilities in sight. And you might wonder how the devil you're going to earn that extra $5,000 or $10,000 that you need. Don't worry; this isn't a serious dilemma. Just fully permeate your unconscious with your goal, duly written down stating such and such an amount and deadline. Your unconscious will do the rest. Then just stay on your toes. Since you've become aware that things won't get better on their own, when an opportunity arises, seize it without the slightest hesitation. Don't let yourself be paralyzed by fear, which prevents so many people from living out their dreams. You know that by doing nothing you won't get your raise. So you mustn't hesitate to take the steps necessary to achieve your goal.

"Correctly programmed, your unconscious will work wonders for you. If you've issued it the order to increase your income by $10,000, it will definitely execute it. Remind it daily, so your mission becomes its magnificent obsession. Like a remote-control missile, it will overcome all the obstacles in its way to hit its target.

"What is the target?" he continued. "When must the explosion take place? The target is $10,000 and the explosion date is a year from now. Such are the magical powers of the unconscious and a quantified objective.

"When creating your objectives, keep in mind that

most people are much too cautious. They don't believe they're worth anything.

"A few years ago," he whispered confidentially to the young man, "I was thinking of hiring a managing director for one of my companies. I worked out that I'd be ready to offer him a salary of $80,000. When the time came to discuss his salary, he told me in a rather nervous, almost imperious voice: 'I won't accept anything below $50,000.'

"After a lengthy pause I said, as if I was making a major concession: 'Given your background, $50,000 is fine by me.'

"If he had asked for $60,000, or $70,000, I'd have given it to him. In fact, the way the interview had gone pleased me so much I might even have bumped that amount up to $100,000.

"So the person I took on lost himself at least $30,000 in a matter of minutes. That's a lot of money. And he lost it simply because he didn't believe he was worth $80,000 a year. I must admit, after hearing him state his salary expectations, I hesitated for a second and considered not hiring him after all. He was in the best position to assess his own worth, and he was telling me that his managerial skills were worth only $50,000 while I was looking for someone worth $80,000. Was I making the wrong choice? The future proved I'd made the right choice by hiring him, and I saved a lot of money. His problem was that he lacked self-confidence and underestimated his worth. He gradually dealt with this problem over the years, and it cost me a bundle in salary increases. But they were worth it.

"What you should remember from this simple example is that I dealt with this manager just as life deals with each of us. Life gives us exactly what we expect from it. No more, no less. We tend to forget, however, that it is generally ready to give us much more than we realize.

"I've talked a lot," said the millionaire. "What do you make of all this, young man?"

"It seems too good to be true," he said.

"Yet this simple little method, and no other," the millionaire responded, "is exactly what helped turn me into a millionaire and has done the same for all those I've shared it with.

"As I've said, words are extremely powerful agents. The stronger your character becomes, the more the words you utter will become genuine decrees. Everything you affirm, fueled by deep inner conviction and strengthened by the fires of repetition, will take shape more and more quickly.

"You have to do the exercise. Nobody can do it for you. You must repeat your formula aloud day and night at least fifty times. And more if you can. Even a hundred times a day. This is an exercise in itself. The first few times I laid down and counted by tapping my fingers on the floor, five times with both hands. It takes practice."

"At first you'll find it won't be easy. The mind is prone to wander. After repeating it ten times, you'll start thinking of something else. Bring your mind back to business and start at zero again until you manage to reach fifty, because if you can't stick to such an elementary form of discipline, you'd better give up your dream of becoming rich.

"That's the challenge I'm offering you, my young friend. And I know you can do it. All you need to do is persist."

"Why repeat the formula aloud?"

"It affects your mind even more strongly. The order you are issuing to your unconscious seems as though it is coming from the outside, and thus sounds more commanding. Say it in a monotone, like an incantation or a mantra, as the Buddhists call it. In time the formula will acquire its own life.

"At first, you might feel a little embarrassed by the sound of your voice and by the formula you're repeating. But gradually you'll get used to it. The goal you laid out for yourself, which seemed audacious at first, will soon appear attainable, even easy to achieve."

"I'm afraid I might feel absolutely ridiculous."

"It's during those moments especially that you must persist. You must conquer your doubt. Think of me, living proof. Even if I'm in a garden far from here, my forces will be with you. In your moments of doubt, remember that I've given you my word. You *will* succeed."

"You're sure about that?" asked the young man, still not totally convinced.

"Why would I have any doubts about it? You'll become an instant millionaire like I did. It's only a matter of time before you become a millionaire in reality. You will soon be one in your mind, and that's what is most important."

"Even without a penny to my name...."

"Keep repeating the formula. Little by little you will see a change occurring within you. Your goal will seem more and more natural. It'll become part of your life in just the same way that the narrow image you have had of yourself until now—a well-worn figment of your imagination—has been an integral part of your being. What your mind conjured up in the past can be reformulated. As such, you will be able to mold your future the way you want it; you will at last become master of your own destiny. Isn't that our secret dream, even before we admit it's possible?"

The young man agreed, and was overwhelmed with emotion at the prospect of mastering his destiny. The old man's words had much greater significance than he had at first believed. Of course his methods were a bit strange. But perhaps they worked.

CHAPTER TWELVE

❧

*In which the young man
learns about happiness and life*

TO HELP AND SUPPORT YOU," the Instant
Millionaire told his young student, "I'll give
you another more general formula. You'll de-
rive enormous benefits from it throughout your
life. It will transform you inside and out. In fact, it
will enable you to acquire *true* wealth—which isn't
only the acquisition of material possessions. True
wealth is much broader than that.

"Your money formula will allow you to achieve and
probably even surpass your financial objectives. But
during your search for wealth, never lose sight of the
fact that if you lose happiness, you lose everything.
The pursuit of money can easily turn into an obses-

sion preventing you from enjoying life. And as the saying goes: 'What shall it profit a man, if he shall gain the whole world, and lose his soul?' Money is an excellent servant but a tyrannical master."

"Do you mean that happiness and money can't coexist?"

"Far from it, but you must stay very alert not to lose your perspective. One of the richest men in the world, John D. Rockefeller, was so preoccupied, so crushed by the weight of his worries, that by the age of fifty he was a little old man. His stomach was so out of order that all it could stand was bread and milk. He lived in constant fear of losing his money and being betrayed by his associates. Money had become his master. He couldn't enjoy it anymore. In a way he was poorer than a simple office clerk who could enjoy a good meal."

"At the same time that you're dangling wealth in front of my eyes," said the young man, "you manage to frighten me as well."

"That's not my intention, though," replied the millionaire, "and the formula I'm about to give you will help you avoid the trap many fortune-seekers have fallen into. People who are still basically poor work relentlessly to achieve their ends. The first money they earn triggers their deep-seated ambition, and causes them to crave more and more. And when they start earning big money they become afraid of losing it.

"It is a formula devised by the famous physician Emile Coué for patients in his clinic: *Every day, in every way, I'm getting better and better*. Repeat this formula aloud fifty times, morning and evening, and as many times as you can during the day. The more often you repeat it, the greater the impact it will have on you."

The young man found himself thinking that the man sitting next to him was the first truly happy man he had ever met in his life.

"Most people want to be happy," said the millionaire, "but they don't know what they're looking for. So inevitably they die without ever having found it. Even if they did find it, how would they recognize it? They're exactly like the people searching for wealth. They truly want to be rich. But when you ask them abruptly how much they'd like to earn in a year, most of them are incapable of answering. When you don't know where you're going, you generally get nowhere."

This made perfect sense to the young man. It was so disarmingly simple, he wondered why he'd never thought of it before. He'd never taken the time to clearly describe what he wanted, to really think things through. He vowed then and there that in the future he would do a lot more thinking, and reflect upon the things that mattered in his life. That would probably prevent a lot of mistakes.

"Happiness, of course, has been defined in countless different ways," the millionaire said. "For each of us, even for those of us who have given it much thought, it translates into a wide variety of things. But I'll give you the key to happiness. With this key you will be able to know beyond a shadow of a doubt at any time of your life if you are happy, if you are doing what it takes to make you happy. Ask yourself this: If I were to die tonight, could I tell myself at the instant of my death that I had accomplished everything I had set out to do that day?

"When you have done exactly what your inner self feels you should do each day, you will feel free to leave the world each day. To be perfectly sure that you are doing what you should be doing, you will have to do what you love doing. People who don't do what they enjoy are not happy. They spend their time daydreaming about what they would like to be doing. And when people aren't happy, they aren't ready to die at a moment's notice."

"I've barely started living, and here you go talking to me about death as if it were just around the corner," the young man said.

"I admit this philosophy may seem morbid at first. And yet it's a philosophy of *life*, one hundred percent. Those who never do what they really enjoy doing, who have given up their dreams, so to speak, belong to the living dead. To really understand what I mean, ask yourself that question and answer it with total sincerity. If you lie, you'll only be lying to yourself, and you become the loser in this game. If you knew you were going to die tomorrow, wouldn't you change your plans for today? Wouldn't you do something else with your life rather than what you've been doing up to now?"

"I'm sure I would."

"You'd probably start by making the necessary arrangements: you'd make a will, if you hadn't already, and say good-bye to your family and friends. But let's suppose that all of these tasks took only one hour.

What would you do with the remaining twenty-three? Ask that question of everybody you know. Their responses will invariably fall into two categories. Unhappy people who don't enjoy their lives will tell you that they'd do something totally different. Why on earth would they continue doing something they hated if they had only twenty-four hours left to live?

"Those in the second category," he continued, "and unfortunately they're the minority, would do exactly what they normally do every day of their lives. Why would they change anything? Their work is their passion. Isn't it quite understandable they would do it until their time was up? Bach belonged to this category. On his deathbed he was correcting his last piece of music. But you don't have to be a genius to want to work until the end. Each of us in our own way and in our own occupation can become a genius, even if unrecognized as such by society. *To be a genius simply means to do what you enjoy doing. That is the true genius of life.* Mediocrity is never daring to do what you love, for fear of what others will say or for fear of losing your security."

"A security that is an illusion more often than not, isn't it?" asked the young man.

"That's right. So ask yourself the question: If I were to die tomorrow, what would I do with the last hours of my life? Would I agree to go on being a shadow of my true self, lacking in self-respect, forcing myself to do something I hate? Imagine you invite a friend over to your house to help you do some chores. Would you give the dirtiest ones to your friend? Of course not. So why force on yourself tasks that you find so degrading? Why be your own worst enemy? Why not become your own best friend?"

There was a moment of silence, and then the old millionaire asked the young man directly, "And what would you do if you were to die tomorrow? Would you do exactly what you've been doing?"

"No, I wouldn't."

"Now, consider the following observation. Don't you find it highly presumptuous to believe that you won't die tomorrow?"

The young man felt troubled. The old man had often displayed an uncanny ability to see into the future—was he now announcing his imminent death? The millionaire seemed to read his thoughts.

"Don't worry," he said, obviously amused, "you're not going to die tomorrow. You'll live to a ripe old age. But allow me to pursue my line of reasoning. Don't you find it presumptuous of people to believe that they always have their entire lives ahead of them? In many cases, death strikes out of the blue. But people create the illusion that they have lots of time ahead of them, and they constantly put off the decisions they should make. They tell themselves: 'I've got time. I'll get down to business later.' Then old age arrives and they find they haven't done anything yet."

"It reminds me of a saying I heard: 'If youth only knew, if old age only could,' " said the young man.

"Exactly! The secret of happiness, therefore, is to live as if each day was your last. And to live each day to the fullest by doing what you want to do. What you would do if your hours were numbered. Because, realistically, they are. We always seem to realize this when there's very little time left. Then it's too late. So *you must be courageous enough to act immediately*. Live with this thought in mind: I refuse to die without having had the courage to do what I wanted to do. I don't want to die with the appalling thought that society tricked me, that it got the better of me and annihilated my dreams. You must not die with the dreadful feeling that your fears were greater than your dreams and that you never discovered what you really enjoy. *You must know how to dare.*"

"I totally agree," said the young man, "but what happens if I'm not absolutely sure that I don't really like what I'm doing? I don't know of any occupation that's completely free of hassles."

"You're absolutely right. Even a profession that fires us up has its negative aspects. But to find out whether your job *really* pleases you, ask yourself this question: If I had a million dollars in the bank, right at this moment, would I continue doing the same job? Obviously, if your answer is no, you don't like it enough. Tell me, how many people would continue in the same occupation if they suddenly became millionaires? They are few and far between. And those who would answer yes to this question are generally already millionaires. Most of the millionaires I know refuse to retire. They go on working very late in life. I'd even go so far as to say that all millionaires, at least all self-made millionaires, made their fortunes precisely because they loved their work.

"My reasoning has just come full circle," the millionaire said. "To become a millionaire, you must enjoy your occupation. Those who stay in a job they hate are doubly penalized. Not only do they despise their work, but, worse yet, it doesn't even make them wealthy. In fact, most people spend their lives in this strange paradox. Why? Because they are unaware of the genuine laws of success, and because of fear. They waste their lives and their chances of becoming truly rich by clinging to a type of security that is mediocre at best. They believe wealth is reserved for others, or that they don't have the necessary talent. And why do they let themselves be tricked into believing these illusions? Because their minds are not conditioned to see reality, to see that their beliefs are an illusion. Remember the saying: 'Character equals destiny.' Strengthen your mind, and circumstances will yield to your desires. You will gain control over your own life."

"Have you always been happy?" asked the young man.

"No, not at all. There were times when I was absolutely miserable. The thought of committing suicide even crossed my mind. But then I, too, met an eccentric old millionaire who taught me almost everything I'm telling you today. At first I was pretty skeptical. I couldn't believe this theory could apply in my case, even though he was living proof that it worked. But since I had tried all sorts of things and was still unsuccessful, and since I had nothing to lose, I was willing to give it a try. I was thirty and I felt I was wasting my life. It seemed as if things were slipping through my fingers."

"I'm sure that today you don't regret having taken that advice."

"He often said I could become the master of my life and control all the events taking place in it. But I never believed him; it seemed like science fiction. Then, one day, after hearing him repeat the same song over and over again, I told myself that maybe he was right. Maybe life was not what I'd always thought it was: a series of more or less unpredictable and uncontrollable events in which luck or fate ruled. Maybe it was possible that we could control our destinies if we mastered our minds. Soon I was beginning to think like that; in other words, a revolution was taking place in my mind. It happened only after I'd spent quite some time repeating to myself: *Every day, in every way, I'm getting better and better.*

"My mentor also taught me another formula, which

in my opinion is even more powerful—at least as far as my own experience goes—and I highly recommend it to you. It's slightly religious in nature, which puts some people off. But that's a pity, since it has an invaluable effect on the mind. Repeating this formula has calmed me down when I felt anxious or nervous and has brought me answers when I seriously needed them. Tranquility is the greatest manifestation of power.

"Be still, and know that I am God. Repeat it every day as often as you can. It will bring you that feeling of serenity so necessary for getting through life's upheavals. When my mentor decided to reveal it to me, he said that of all the secrets in the world, this one was the most precious. It was his spiritual legacy to me, as it is mine to you.

"By repeating this formula, which seemed strange to me at first, I developed a new inner power. This power, which never ceased growing over the years, kept reminding me of something the old millionaire had repeated to me over and over again: *I could do anything,* nothing would be impossible for me as soon as I became the master of my destiny. So, little by little, I convinced myself that I could steer my life

exactly where I wanted it to go. I've continued applying the formula and I want you to do the same thing."

CHAPTER THIRTEEN

***

*In which the young man
learns to express
his desires in life*

YOU HAVE ALREADY taken the first step," explained the millionaire, "writing the formula and the quantified objective: an amount and a deadline. Now for the second step: take a sheet of paper and write down everything you want out of life. Your dream must be precise if you want it to take shape. I'll show you what I asked for in the beginning. It was many years ago, so I'll translate the amounts into today's dollars:

"The following financial goals within five years:
- A house worth $500,000.
- A second home in the country worth $300,000.

- A new BMW worth $60,000.
- An old, rebuilt Mercedes worth $40,000.
- No more personal debts.
- $300,000 in cash and other liquid assets.
- $300,000 invested in the stock market and other investments.
- $500,000 invested in property, which grows to $3,000,000 in equity within five years from the time of purchase.

"My non-financial objectives were:
- Two-week vacations at least three times a year, whenever I felt like taking them.
- To be my own boss and not work more than thirty hours a week.
- Intelligent friends involved in business and art.
- A loving and charming wife and beautiful children; a fulfilling family life.
- A maid and cook to free us of everyday tasks."

The young man was overwhelmed by the picture the Instant Millionaire had just drawn.

"It looks too good to be true, doesn't it?" said the millionaire. "I too thought that I'd gone a bit overboard by the time I'd finished outlining what I wanted. But my hesitation and fears were due to a negative mental attitude and my ingrained habit of thinking small. I was doing this without even realizing it.

"Making out a list like this is exactly the way to discover your narrow vision of things. Those who consider this kind of life plan unachievable simply think small. Everything being relative under the sun, this ambition is hardly exorbitant. Most wealthy people would be exceedingly unhappy if they had to make do with the paltry conditions I have just sketched out. Many of them live in houses worth millions, employ dozens of servants, and own ranches, private planes, tropical islands, racehorses, and so on. Many of them don't even think they're rich! In any case not *that* rich, since they always have friends or business associates with more money than they have.

"Why do they find this kind of lifestyle natural? Well, they were either born rich, or they thought big and managed to achieve their dreams. They never believed that they couldn't do it. If you start out with the idea that you can't, you immediately block yourself.

"So, do this exercise. Write down what you want out of life in minute detail, without holding anything back. It will show you the limits of your ambitions and your mentality. What are you really dreaming of? What would you be satisfied with? It's important to fill in as many details as possible. The only thing to avoid is choosing your dream home at a specific address, because that particular house may never be available and you'd be running the risk of never seeing your dream come true despite the power of your desire and will. But other than that, be as specific as possible.

"There's one other important thing to consider, and that is the possibility that your dream is harmful to others. Always keep in mind that if your goals are harmful to anyone, they must be avoided for your own good as well as for the good of others.

"This portrait will show you who you really are. It will become the concrete shape of your desires. Your thoughts are alive. The more specific your portrait, the better the chances are for it to materialize. Details are very important. In mysterious and unexpected ways your thoughts, nourished regularly, bring about the circumstances that allow them to become reality."

The young man looked a bit skeptical.

"I know all this seems Utopian," the millionaire

said. "But as I told you, the stronger your mind be-comes, the more you realize there's nothing it can't accomplish. Miracles happen. Don't you find that, comparatively speaking, realizing a dream as ordi-nary as having a $500,000 house is a rather banal achievement? Don't you believe that the mind is much more powerful than many people think and above all believe it to be? Remember what Christ said: 'Faith moves mountains.'

"To use your mind effectively, you've got to start believing in its power, or at least be open to the possibility that it might be as powerful as I'm telling you it is. So draw up your list."

"I need time to think," said the young man.

"That's good. Think about what I've just told you. Part of you believes what I'm saying. A highly crea-tive part of you has been blinded by years of faulty education and unfortunate experiences, but it's still alive. It's only waiting for a sign from you, and it will show you how to become the lord and master of your existence instead of a tormented slave helplessly buf-feted by events. To do that you must learn to listen to that tiny inner voice sleeping in the depths of your mind and give it more freedom to express itself. This is your intuition, the voice of your soul. It's the way to your secret power. The more often you repeat the formula, *Be still, and know that I am God*, the more powerful your inner voice will become and the more surely it will guide you."

The young man felt a bit overloaded; he was ready to take a break.

"Come," said the millionaire, "let's relax and take a walk in the garden. I'd love to take my last walk here with a friend."

These somber words saddened the young man. It wasn't the first time he had made such an allusion....

CHAPTER FOURTEEN

~

*In which the young man
discovers the secrets
of the rose garden*

T HE TWO MEN walked through the garden in
silence until the millionaire stopped in front
of a rose bush laden with magnificent flowers.

"I must have smelled these roses thousands of times, and yet each time it's a different
experience. Do you know why? Because I've learned
to live in the here and now, and not dwell on the past
or the future. It's a matter of mental concentration—
focusing, contemplation, meditation—a great many
words have been used to describe it. The more you
concentrate on what you are doing, absorbed in the
task or object or person in front of you, the more you
live in the present. This focus, this concentration, is

a key to success in all facets of life. The better your concentration, the more quickly and efficiently you're able to work. You'll spot details that others overlook."

"Have all rich and successful people learned to pay attention to details?"

"They have indeed. By increasing your own powers of concentration, you will be able to make wise observations. You will learn to judge accurately the people you meet. Your powers of concentration will enable you to discover at a glance who they really are. And you will become realistic in the truest sense of the word: You will see things as they are.

"Most people go through life constantly distracted, like sleepwalkers. They don't really *see* things or *see* the people they meet. They live as if in a dream. They are never in the present. Their mistakes and failures haunt them. Their minds are filled with fears of the future."

"I have a feeling that concentration, as you're describing it, is quite a difficult thing to achieve."

"It takes practice, and not everyone who tries it succeeds. But when your mind reaches a proper level of concentration, your ability to solve problems becomes formidable. You can leap over problems most people dwell on. Instead of wasting your nervous energy biting your nails over your worries, you apply yourself to resolving them. Being overanxious never solved anything—it simply provoked many a stomach ulcer and heart attack.

"As you develop your forces of concentration, the image you have of yourself will change. Each human being is an enigma; unfortunately, many of us are enigmas not only to others, but to ourselves as well. This comes from a lack of concentration."

The young man was listening intently.

"Given concentration, you will understand why you've been placed where you are in the world, in this exact spot. This will appear clearer and clearer to you, more and more obvious. Your mind will be penetrated by very calming, reassuring thoughts, and you'll find yourself realizing, as if waking up after a long, deep sleep, 'Ah! That's who I am. That's why I'm here at this moment. That's why I'm with this person. That's why I'm doing what I'm doing.' You'll experience what could be called a feeling of destiny. You'll understand your destiny. And a feeling of acceptance will come into play. That doesn't mean you resign yourself to fate; it means you will see with clear-sighted vision the position you're in right now, you'll accept it, and you'll recognize it as your personal starting point. This will guide your career and allow you to take the reins of your destiny firmly in your hands."

The millionaire took a moment to bend down and inhale the perfume of the rose.

"The rose is a symbol of life. The thorns represent the road of experience: the trials and tribulations each one of us must undergo to understand the true beauty of existence."

He pulled a pair of pruning shears out of his pocket, snipped a rose, and offered it to his young companion.

"Keep this rose with you," he said. "It will act as a talisman and bring you good luck. Lady Luck exists. Trust in her. Caress her with your thoughts. Ask her for what you want and she will respond. All successful people believe in luck, in one form or another.

"With this simple rose, you are an initiate. You belong to the Order of the Rose. Each time you feel the need, find this rose. It will give you strength. And each time you have doubts about yourself, each time life seems too difficult to bear, come back to this symbolic rose and remember what it represents.

Each ordeal, each problem, each mistake will one day be transformed into a magnificent petal.

"Each day, set aside some time to concentrate on the heart of the rose. Repeat calmly to yourself: *Be still, and know that I am God*. Contemplate the rose for longer and longer periods of time while repeating this. When you are able to do it for twenty minutes, your concentration will be much improved.

"When your heart becomes like the rose, your life will be transformed."

The young man breathed in the delicate scent of the rose.

"Let me repeat what I have said, so you are sure to remember. When your mind has become strong and self-assured through concentration exercises, you will come to realize that life's problems no longer have any hold over you. You will understand that things are only as important as the mind believes them to be. A problem is a problem only if you make it a problem.

"The stronger your mind is, the more insignificant your problems appear. This is the source of inner peace, so *concentrate*. This is one of the greatest keys to success.

"All of life is an exercise in strengthening the mind.

The soul is immortal. We pass from life to life, and the mind slowly discovers itself and develops. This apprenticeship is generally a long one. And people who have no more than modest success in reaching their goals have yet to achieve high levels of concentration. Perhaps not all successful people have made it a point to practice specific concentration exercises. But over the course of many lives on earth they have achieved a level of concentration that allowed them to succeed more easily than others. When your mind reaches its highest level of concentration, you will enter that extraordinary state where dreams and reality coincide."

The millionaire and the young man began walking back to the house. The sky became dark and cloudy, casting shadows over the mansion. When they entered the dining room, the old man lit a candelabra. Then he went to the window, pulled the curtain back, and glanced up toward the sky.

"Always remember that at a certain height there are no clouds. If there are clouds in your life, it's because your soul hasn't soared high enough.

"Many people make the mistake of fighting against their problems. What you must do is raise yourself above those problems once and for all. The heart of the rose will lead you above the clouds, where the sky is forever clear. Don't waste your time chasing the clouds, they will unceasingly reappear...."

The millionaire and the young man sat down at the dinner table. The butler arrived, bringing bread and wine.

"I've been wondering about something for quite a while," said the young man. "I do think everything you've been saying is true. And I now believe that if I apply the formulas you've given me, I can become a millionaire quickly and even attain peace of mind. But I still wonder about the *field* in which I'll be able to make a fortune."

His concern apparently amused the millionaire.

"You must put your trust in life and in the power of your mind," he said. "Don't worry. First set your goal, then ask your deep unconscious to steer you toward the path that will lead to riches. Start by asking; then wait. The answer won't be long in coming."

The young man was disappointed. He wanted something a little more specific.

The millionaire winced in sympathy and quickly

added: "You must find work that is satisfying to your heart. Think about it. All the elements of the occupation that will please you are already within you. You simply don't recognize them because you aren't yet in tune with your true nature. As you continue to concentrate, to meditate more and more, you will connect with your true essence, and every answer you need will be revealed to you. And best of all, you will discover what most people desperately seek all of their lives and never find: the mysterious purpose of your existence on earth. And you will understand it not only with your head but with your heart as well.

"You have everything to gain from concentrating on the heart of the rose. There you will find the be-all and end-all of your existence. In time, you will realize this."

He stopped for a moment and took a tiny sip of wine; delicately savoring it. His eyes were closed in a kind of religious reverence.

"I know I would like to start a business of some kind," said the young man, "but where would I get the money to start, I haven't got a dime?"

"How much would you need?"

"I don't know—at least $25,000. That's how much you needed to start."

"You should be able to find it. Look around a little. What possibilities can you think of?"

"I can't think of any. I don't know of any bank that would give me a loan. I have no collateral. I have very little left over from my salary at the end of the month, and I don't own anything, except my car, which isn't worth anything...."

"Can't you at least think of something to try? Somewhere to begin?"

"Not really...."

"That's a mistake you should never repeat. Don't be like so many people, who give up before they even try. That's the best way of never doing anything and never succeeding at anything. And don't fall into the same trap as those who take action but are inwardly convinced that they won't succeed. Bring your thoughts and actions into harmony. Be in harmony with yourself."

"I'm willing all right, but I just don't see any possibilities."

"You must start out firmly convinced that the solution exists—the ideal solution to your problem. The power of your mind and the magic of your objective will invariably attract the solution to you in ways you don't even suspect exist. Be inwardly convinced that you will succeed, and you will. Don't leave room for doubt. Banish it with all the strength your mind can muster. Doubt and optimism are in constant conflict. Struggle staunchly against doubt, for doubt, like all thoughts, tends to materialize in your life. If you are firmly convinced that you will get your loan, you will.

"In your present circumstances, what would you do to reach your goal—that is, to get a loan?"

"I don't really know."

"If you only had a short time—let's say an hour—to get $25,000 to set up your own business, what would you do?"

"I... I have no idea...."

"Standing before you is a millionaire who has just encouraged you, given you the secrets of his success, and you don't know what to do? Not one thing comes to mind to get this money?"

It suddenly dawned on the young man. Perhaps all

he needed to do was ask the millionaire for the money. He hesitated a moment, then took a deep breath.

"Would you lend me the $25,000 I need?"

"There you go. Now, wasn't that easy? All you had to do was ask. People seldom dare to ask. *You must dare to make a request.*"

The millionaire pulled out the $25,000 he kept as pocket money. He cast a nostalgic glance at the thick pile of cash and then handed it over to the young man, who accepted it, tremulous with emotion. He had never held such a vast sum of money in his life.

"There's absolutely no reason why acquiring money in the future should be any more difficult for you than it has been for me," said the old man. "It's unfortunate that it's so commonly believed that money is hard to come by and that you have to work hard to get it. In fact, the value of work is to strengthen the fiber of your mind. When you have earned a lot of money—and I assure you it won't be long in coming if you apply the secrets I've taught you—you will realize that what counts is your mental attitude, the power of your desire, and being able to channel that power by means of a specific monetary objective. Don't forget that outside circumstances always end up reflecting the state of your mind and the nature of your innermost convictions."

The young man was so overcome with joy at having $25,000 in his hands that he wasn't fully listening to the millionaire's words of advice.

"Remember, young man, when you need money, if you are positive you can get it easily and quickly, you will. And as soon as doubt begins to invade your mind, think back to the $25,000 you've just obtained. All you need to do is ask. If you are convinced that you will get what you ask for at the very moment you ask, if you act as if it is already yours, you will get it.

"When you do have doubts, apply some self-suggestion. Turn your words into commands. When your mind has become powerful enough, each suggestion will become a royal decree. Your words and reality will become one. And the time it takes for your commands to materialize will become briefer and briefer, and finally instantaneous.

"And you must never forget to consider the good of others at all times, so that the power of your words doesn't turn against you."

He paused again.

"This money," he went on, pointing to the thick wad of bills, "well, I'm not lending it to you...."

He hesitated a second, and seemed amused by the young man's startled reaction.

"I'm not lending it to you. I'm giving it to you. By doing so, everything will have come full circle. It was given to me by my mentor to start me out in business. Don't use it for any other reason. And don't imitate the man in the Bible who buried his coins instead of letting them work for him. Don't let fear be your guide. Fear is your worst enemy, the brother of doubt, and you must conquer it. Be fearless and bold. Anyone who, under the pretext of caution or rationality, buries the money he has received is not worthy of it, and it's highly unlikely that he will get more. Money must flow freely to be able to multiply.

"The money I'm giving you is, however, at heart a loan," the millionaire continued. "One day you, in turn, must give it to someone else. Many years from now you will meet someone in the same situation you are in now. You'll recognize him intuitively. You must give him the equivalent of what this amount represents today. Then he, too, may start out with a substantial amount. Make sure that by then it represents an insignificant amount to you: pocket money and no more."

The young man was filled with gratitude. He agreed to the terms, and thanked the old man warmly.

"There's one more thing you must know..."

As he said this, it began to pour. The millionaire watched the rain with a somber expression. "All the signs are coming to pass," he muttered to himself. Then he addressed the young man again.

"As I said, there's one more thing you need to know: The secrets I have passed on to you are effective for reaching *all* of the goals you will set for yourself. The reason I amassed such a colossal fortune is not that money interested me so much. It was a way to show men and women of little faith the power of the mind.

"Our greatest possession is freedom, and wealth can give you freedom. It'll be good for you to know this freedom. With it, you will see many an illusion vanish. You'll also understand that true freedom is found in detachment. Only he who leaves with empty hands will be able to tend the eternal roses. Achieving this freedom was the goal of my entire existence.

Despite what others thought, I have never been anything other than a humble gardener."

"Why have you told *me* all these things?" the young man asked. "Why have you given *me* this money? You certainly didn't owe me anything. It could easily have been somebody else who came to see you...."

"But that's just it—no one else came. Your desire led you to me. This is what happens in life. Hasn't it been said that once the disciple is ready, the master appears?"

The millionaire smiled. His somber and distant expression disappeared; he looked at the young man affectionately.

"The soul is eternal. And each soul travels from one life to another surrounded by companions, each helping another to fulfill his destiny. The encounters we have during our lifetime are never the result of coincidence."

The millionaire approached him regally. His face almost seemed to glow with a light of its own. He lightly touched the young man on the forehead with his right index finger, and said, "Discover who you really are. The truth will forever set you free."

Outside, the storm subsided as quickly as it had

begun, and the sun burst forth brightly again. The old man picked up the candelabra and carried it away without saying another word.

The young man found himself alone, his head teeming with thoughts, holding the money the millionaire had given him.

CHAPTER FIFTEEN

❧

*In which the young man
and the old man
embark on different journeys*

THE YOUNG MAN was not alone for long. The butler appeared, holding an envelope. He handed it to the young man and said, "My master entrusted me with the task of giving this to you. He said you should read it in the privacy of your room. You can spend another day here. Then you must go. These are my master's wishes."

The young man thanked him and went immediately to his room. This time, however, he took the precaution of leaving the door slightly open....

The envelope was sealed with red wax in the shape of a rose. The young man sat on the edge of the bed and carefully broke open the seal. A delicate scent of roses wafted from it. He pulled out the Instant Millionaire's will.

This extraordinary testament was handwritten in ample, majestic letters that seemed to breathe as if imbued with their own life. A beautifully handwritten letter accompanied it, written in black ink.

"These are my last requests," he read. "I am leaving you all the books in my library. Some people believe that books are utterly worthless. They believe that they themselves are reinventing the world. And since they have not benefitted from the knowledge found in books, they unfortunately repeat the mistakes made by their forefathers. In this way, they waste a lot of time and a lot of money.

"On the other hand, don't fall into the trap of trusting implicitly in what books contain, letting those who came before you do your thinking for you. Retain only what outlasts the passage of time.

"Since our first encounter, I have tried to convey to you the pearls of wisdom I have been able to glean during my long life. In this document you will find a few thoughts that represent my spiritual legacy. I would like you to do your best to communicate them to as many people as you can. Tell people about our encounter and the secrets you have learned. Before doing so, however, you must try them out. A method that has not been tested and proven is completely worthless.

"Within six years you will be a millionaire. At that time you will be free to undertake the steps necessary to share this legacy with people.

"Now I must leave you. My roses are waiting."

The young man was choked with emotion, and sat for a moment in silence.

He wanted to thank the millionaire for having given him such precious gifts. He went quickly back to the dining room, but found no one. He called out to the butler, but there was no answer.

He ran out to the garden and spotted the millionaire lying in the middle of a path at the foot of a rose bush.

"How eccentric," thought the young man, "sleeping in the middle of a garden." But the nearer he drew the more troubled he became.

The old man's hands were folded upon his chest, and he held a single rose. His face was perfectly serene.

Had he known the exact moment he was going to

die? Had he chosen the moment of his departure, and simply willed himself to die?

It was one secret the millionaire had taken with him.

The young man sensed it was time for him, too, to leave. He reached to take the rose, but then pulled his hand away. That rose belonged to the Instant Millionaire. It was his final companion.

He stood over the millionaire and vowed to convey his teachings as best he could, then started down the path to return home.

When the millionaire's library was delivered to his apartment, it was so immense it left little room for the rest of his things. He was confronted with a dilemma: either move elsewhere or get rid of some of the books. He chose to move. And he did it with a light heart.

Epilogue

JUST AS THE MILLIONAIRE had predicted, the young man made his first million before his six-year deadline was up. And he kept his promise: He took a month off and wrote about his encounter with the Instant Millionaire and the life-giving philosophy he had passed on to him.

HOW TO
THINK LIKE
— A —

CONTENTS

Author's Preface

—ᴗ—

by MARK FISHER
Author of *The Instant Millionaire*

OVER THE YEARS, enthusiastic readers from all over the world have written me many wonderful letters. Most of them ask me about *The Instant Millionaire*'s formula to become rich and happy.

I've tried my best to answer their questions, but I have not been able to answer all the letters in as much detail and as thoughtfully as I would like. I often thought about this problem, and even meditated on it as I contemplated the heart of a Queen Elizabeth rose — my favorite! — that grows in my garden....

One day, a solution came to me: I would write

one long letter that would attempt to answer all the questions I had been asked. The letter grew and grew, as I kept adding to it over a period of nearly three years. It got so long that it was too lengthy to easily duplicate — and I realized I had a book-length manuscript on my hands.

I sent it to my publisher — and friend — Marc Allen, who had just written a very impressive and inspiring book, *Visionary Business: An Entrepreneur's Guide to Success*. Marc was so enthusiastic about all my notes that he wanted to not only publish them, but to add a lot of his ideas as well. We collaborated back and forth for several months, through several drafts, and he added so much that I felt he deserved credit as a coauthor. And Becky Benenate, editorial director of New World Library, added quite a bit as well, as a highly supportive and capable editor.

The result was exciting: Two self-made millionaires from very different backgrounds writing back and forth, attempting to summarize every valuable piece of advice we have ever received, and everything we have put into practice, into a single, concise work.

It has certainly evolved far beyond my initial

idea! With every addition, every rewrite, it grew stronger and stronger, until it was something I feel honored and proud to have published. I hope you will find it to be a powerful and practical tool to help you truly succeed — in any and every way you choose to define success.

One can never consent to creep
when one feels an impulse to soar.

— HELEN KELLER

Introduction

—⁓—

SUCCESS IS AN ATTITUDE. Success is a habit. Success is easily available to all who want it, *believe* they can have it, and put their desires into action.

Success has no secrets. Many who achieve it readily tell their story of devoting years to their work, to their passion and dreams, before they finally became successful. The main theme is always the same, in every case: *They love their work.* They would have done it anyway. Great fortunes — or at least some level of financial stability and success — were often part of the dream, but the wealth was a by-product of following their passion.

Could you imagine Steven Spielberg making a million dollars a day if he hated movies and funny-looking extraterrestrials? What if Henry Ford hadn't been fascinated with machinery? If Donna Karan hated clothes? When we do what we love, offering our gifts and talents, without causing harm to anyone, we are working at the highest level of service for ourselves, those around us, and our planet.

Success can't be attributed to fate, but to the deliberate application of very specific principles. Luck may be involved, but only because, as has been said, luck occurs when preparation meets opportunity.

Age, education, money, background, and childhood experience do not matter in the face of these principles. The childhoods of the world's richest self-made millionaires, successful artists, and noted performers were many times rather commonplace, often poor, and sometimes miserable. At school, many of them were considered slow learners. Yet, each one of them, at a crucial moment in their lives, decided to take their fate into their own hands and, enlightened by a book, by the word or example of another, or by a powerful sense of intuition, set out to be successful.

You may have reached that critical point that will change your life. No matter how old you are or what circumstances you may be in, all you have to do is be alert and receptive — and believe. Know that it's possible to start from scratch — as so many others have done — and achieve even your loftiest goals. It's just a matter of believing it is possible and becoming determined to create the life you desire.

In our instant-gratification society, we often look only at the final product: the movie star, the millionaire, the acclaimed artist. It looks like overnight success. We don't see the years of dedication and patient persistence that went into the process. Dustin Hoffman joked that it took him ten years to become an overnight success. And Ray Kroc, the founder of McDonald's, wrote in his autobiography, "I was an overnight success all right, but thirty years is a long, long night."

A very important aspect of successful people is that they all had failures, sometimes many failures. Most people never reach success because they give up after one or two setbacks. Napoleon Hill's classic *Think and Grow Rich* recounts the story of a miner who gave up after months of prospecting — three feet from the gold. But he applied this lesson to everything in his life thereafter and eventually became very successful.

As we approach the new millennium, success takes on a new meaning. Fewer people are interested in maintaining a workaholic fever to achieve millions while sacrificing health and home life. Success and prosperity now certainly include a balanced life: performing satisfying work while maintaining fitness and health, having loving relationships and a happy family life, being involved in social activities and causes, and having a sense of inner peace and fulfillment. In a recent *New York Times* poll, most people surveyed said it was more important to them to slow down, work less, and spend more time with friends and family than to pursue more prestige and possessions.

True success can include all of this. Presenting our passionate work to the world is a service to all those around us. Building beautiful relationships and having the time to relish them is an ambition anyone can achieve, if they choose to. Well-thought-out work habits — most importantly the habits of mind — can bring financial security and wealth. With wealth, we have greater freedom to pursue what we enjoy, as well as to give back to the world and help others.

An old Chinese proverb says that a journey of a thousand miles begins with one step. By deciding to read this book you have just taken the first step toward success and living your dreams. Everything in life is a matter of choice. The purpose of this book is not only to help you clarify the options open to you so that you can discover what you really want, but also to help you to achieve those goals.

Perhaps, like so many others, you're unemployed, underemployed, misemployed, or otherwise dissatisfied with your present job. Despite what you may think, despite the "hard times" we are experiencing (that oft-repeated, age-old fallacy, as we shall see further on), despite unemployment and inflation, you can find the ideal job you dream of — faster than you ever believed possible. In spite of the fact that most people presume you can't always do everything you want to in life, you can find a career that will truly satisfy you. It is your right, after all. Your poverty, ill health, loneliness, and misery serve absolutely no one.

A word of warning: Quite often you'll find advice on developing entrepreneurship and setting up a business. This isn't meant to encourage you to drop everything you are doing and go into business for yourself. Not everyone is cut out for this. You need a certain type of personality, and you have to feel a real need to go out on your own. If you feel this urge, then you probably already have the basic qualities of an entrepreneur. This book can be a guide. But even if you aren't the entrepreneurial type, this book will still show you how to improve your position in life, your material assets, and your outlook, without compromising your basic security.

Some of these principles might seem original and surprising, others might seem commonplace. Don't let appearances deceive you. Success depends on them. Don't be put off by the apparent simplicity of some of these golden rules. The most obvious ideas are sometimes the most difficult to incorporate into our daily routine. Take some time to think them over. Are you applying them already? Are they part of your life and working habits?

Read this book *slowly*. Stop and reflect often on the words, and apply them to your life's experience. There is repetition in this book: These simple truths must be repeated, again and again, until we understand them consciously and, even more importantly, until our subconscious mind absorbs them and acts on them. Then we see great changes happening in our lives.

"Give me a point of support," said Archimedes, describing a lever, "and I will lift the world." To achieve success, you need leverage. Here, in this book, is the leverage and support to achieve your dreams.

Chapter 1

Where Do I Start?

The secret of getting ahead is getting started.
The secret of getting started is breaking your
complex overwhelming tasks into small manageable
tasks, and then starting on the first one.

— MARK TWAIN

SOCRATES, THE GREEK PHILOSOPHER, was profoundly aware of the weakness in his own nature. Yet, he came to realize that people are evolving beings, capable of changing and growing toward an ideal. People can always improve themselves. That is part of our greatness. And that ability to improve ourselves can develop at any moment in life.

BELIEVE YOU CAN BE SUCCESSFUL

You have to believe you can be successful before you will ever succeed. Sounds like a cliche, doesn't it? But take time to stop and think about it. Where else can you begin? *Your beliefs create your life experience* — it's not the other way around. And no matter what you believed before, you can change your beliefs and change your life. It's impossible to create success without believing — deeply — that you are capable of being successful. It's impossible to live abundantly without believing that you deserve abundance. Our education, society, and other forms of mental conditioning are all, unfortunately, more pessimistic than optimistic. How often has someone told you not to waste your time on pipe dreams, that you have to be realistic, that you can't have what you want? Because we hear this so often and, as a result, believe it to be true, wealth always seems reserved for the fortunate few. Success seems an exclusive party to which we are cordially not invited.

But this is simply not true. If success and prosperity are an exclusive club, it's because they are so in the minds of people whose attitudes bar their own entry. Every successful person at some point came to believe that one day he or she would be successful.

Your beliefs about success are, no doubt,

deeply ingrained, and you have to be open to changing them before you'll ever succeed. Examine your beliefs to see how they have affected your life. Many people needlessly sabotage themselves because of unexamined "core beliefs" about how the world operates. Marc Allen sums it up in *Visionary Business*:

It's important — in some cases *critically* important — to regularly take time to examine our lives. The first thing to do is to take a look at our past — as clearly and honestly as we can — and discover the important events and influences that have shaped our lives.... Some of these shaping events have led to very good core beliefs — and those moments should be remembered, and those beliefs should be encouraged and supported. All of us have had someone in our lives who saw our potential and supported us in one way or another. We've all had glimpses of our genius, as children, and we've all had other forces that have sought to crush our genius, through doubt, through cynicism, through lack of faith.

We need to reflect on these things occasionally. Those shaping moments that have had a negative impact on us need to be looked at, and we need to discover the negative core beliefs we formed as a result. Once those beliefs are identified, they can be let go of. Because they aren't true — they're simply self-fulfilling things that become true if we believe them. This is the process of becoming conscious — becoming aware of the forces that drive us, and learning how to act on those forces, how to shape our destiny, how to become powerful. How to achieve what we want in life.

What are your beliefs about success? Don't be afraid to analyze your thoughts more closely; you may be surprised at the barriers you have put between yourself and success, once you think about it. When you realize that you can change even your most deeply held beliefs, you can come to see that not only is it possible for you to become as successful as you would like — in all areas of your life — but also that it's easy, much easier than you have ever dreamed possible. In fact, dozens of opportunities appear to you every day. Profitable ideas flash through your mind, but you usually let them slip away without pursuing them with concrete action. The art of self-suggestion, which is discussed throughout this book, helps you discover how to develop your powers of intuition — the sixth sense for success. You already have these qualities, but may not be fully aware of their existence. You only need to access them — and you can, quite easily.

Succeeding Is No Harder than Failing

For most people, failure has become a way of life. Failure is a hard habit to break; after all, our social climate has given us high expectations but our social conditioning has given us low morale. It's a vicious cycle. In order to become successful, we have to understand that *success is basically no more difficult than failure.* It's simply a different kind of mental programming, one to which our subconscious mind is not inherently opposed.

Doesn't every failure involve a highly complex combination of circumstances? Consider what it takes to miss perfect opportunities, to misfire every time you attempt something, to avoid meeting the people who can help you on your path of success, to dismiss your ideas as useless when they could lead to something worthwhile, and to continually repeat the motions that lead to defeat. It's quite an achievement to fail, and yet the subconscious mind accepts defeat as natural. Throughout this book, we analyze the vital role the subconscious plays in manifesting success. When we understand how to get the power of our subconscious mind working on success rather than failure, we will succeed. It is inevitable.

We create all sorts of excuses to block our success. How many of these creep into your thoughts?

• *Everything was much easier in the good old days!*

This excuse is proven wrong every single day of the year. While negative, shortsighted people drone on about unemployment and downsizing, thousands of small businesses start and flourish every year. Thousands — globally, *millions* — of people become millionaires each year! Think of the movies produced, the books published, the new opportunities in computer science and interactive media! Think of the parts of the world that are opening to free trade! Becoming successful is not only possible today, it's actually easier than it used to be. The entire world is ours to offer new ideas, products, services — whatever gift we have to give. Success depends far less on outside circumstances than on our mental attitude, our beliefs about ourselves and the world.

• *I'm too young!*

Tell this to Debbie Fields, founder and owner of Mrs. Fields Cookies, who was in her twenties when she achieved success, or Steve Jobs, founder of Apple Computers, who made his first million when he was twenty-three, his first ten million at twenty-four, and his first 100 million at twenty-five. There is an old saying: "A youth with a single aim in life arrives early at the harvest." Youth is more often than not an asset. Lack of experience can be compensated for by boldness, daring, instinct, and originality. History shows that most successful people started out completely inexperienced and learned as they went along.

- *I'm too old!*

Colonel Sanders and Georgia O'Keefe would disagree. Napoleon Hill's survey of the wealthy showed that many successful people don't reach their goals until midlife and beyond. It could be that this is the time of reaping the benefits of a series of earlier efforts, while many others are thinking of retirement. Work does not kill. Idleness, on the other hand, is often deadly; people who take early retirement often die younger than those who keep working. The fact remains that many people begin a second or third career, sometimes the most successful of all, late in life. Age is irrelevant. Your years of experience, even if you have failed, are priceless to you.

- *I have no capital!*

Most people don't, in the beginning. Money isn't essential when we start out. A good creative idea or business idea and a positive mental outlook are essential. Everyone in the world has at least one talent, one passion, one hobby that can become profitable if applied correctly. Contrary to popular belief, there is no shortage of money in the world.

The money for launching ideas and furthering good in our world is always available.

Poverty seems to be a tradition in far too many families, an inherited trait like the color of one's hair or eyes, passed down from generation to generation. It's often more difficult for people whose families have always been poor to imagine that one day they can become rich. The image we get of ourselves and of life in general is often tinged with hopelessness and pessimism, and the role models that surround us are not always very inspiring. But there are so many exceptions to this — look at Charlie Chaplin, for example, one of history's wealthiest actors. He spent his youth in poverty, wandering the streets of London. The humiliation of poverty and early contact with life's harsh realities have in many cases spurred people on to great achievement.

- *I'm not educated!*

Neither was fashion designer Donna Karan. Thomas Edison left school before the age of sixteen. Microsoft's Bill Gates is a college dropout.

Even though many successful people weren't educated in the formal sense, however, they *did* acquire an in-depth knowledge of the industry in which they made their fortunes.

- *Don't I need an inborn talent?*

No. Many successful people displayed no early signs of being destined for fame, fortune, and fulfillment. Paul Getty said, "I most certainly was not a born businessman." Many people talk themselves into believing that they don't have a special talent or what it takes to change their lives. They go to great lengths to justify their lack of success. And yet, everyone in the world has some talent, some kind of gift. Once we discover our own unique gift, it becomes our purpose to develop it.

- *I don't have the energy it takes!*

This is often an important difference between those who succeed and those who fail: our level of energy. Every action we take requires a minimum amount of energy, especially mental or psychic energy. Low vitality inevitably breeds low motivation. This appears to be another inescapable vicious cycle. But all it takes is a tiny spark to ignite the resources of energy that lie dormant within us. The potential energy we all have is enormous. In many people, it is hibernating, waiting to be activated.

Yet, at the same time, it takes much more energy to do something we don't like than something we enjoy. Think of the energy you have and how time slips away when you're absorbed in your favorite project. When we do what truly interests and motivates us, the energy flows easily and effortlessly.

- *I'm afraid of failure!*

We're born with two fears: falling and loud noises. All other fears are acquired. Unfortunately, the fear of failure is powerful and widespread — and it is paralyzing. Often deeply embedded within us, it results from past failures, from a lack of confidence bred unknowingly by our parents, and it's enforced by society's general negative, short-sighted thinking.

The fear of failure is sometimes expressed overtly but is most often unconscious and subtly disguised. People don't admit they're afraid of failing; instead, they denigrate others for building castles in the air, and they scorn dreams and creative ideas. They're champion excuse-makers: family obligations, problems, lack of time, lack of money. But wouldn't the family prefer a spouse or parent who is content with their work? Wouldn't time be better spent in creative expression? Wouldn't creating fulfillment resolve many problems?

Then there are the "if only" people: If only their boss would notice them.... If only they could find a good idea.... If only they had more talent, ability, time, money, or luck.... If only they had been born in different circumstances, or under another astrological sign....

Obviously, if you never try anything, chances are you will never fail. But then, you're not likely to succeed either. Success doesn't miraculously appear out of the blue. It's always the result of concrete action and a positive mental attitude. Thomas Edison made 10,000 attempts before perfecting the incandescent lightbulb. Abraham Lincoln lost eighteen elections before becoming President of the United States. We're not singing the praises of failure, but we know through experience that every personal defeat can be an education in itself, at least if it's accepted with an open mind.

- *All I've done is fail!*

One underlying reason for many people's paralyzing fear of failure is that they have already failed, or at least believe they were unsuccessful in the past. Each new setback reinforces this feeling and undermines their self-confidence. People start with one failure and see themselves as losers, and this in turn leads inevitably to more aborted attempts. These failures reinforce their loser mentality, and soon it becomes habitual. They end up believing that life is a series of hard knocks, defeats, struggles, and frustrations.

Why have you failed until now? Maybe you wanted to — at least on some level, possibly subconsciously. If the success you're entitled to always slips through your fingers, ask yourself why you've condemned yourself to mediocrity. And reassure yourself that even the strongest, most powerful negative programming can be changed — quickly and completely.

Once you examine it closely, you may be surprised at your inner resistance to success. You may be surprised at your negative inner monologue, which most people relentlessly repeat out of habit.

Here's an important point: Your mind is always working for your welfare — it just may be working for a long outmoded goal. For instance, maybe your high energy or enthusiasm for something as a child brought harsh criticism from your parents or siblings. You very quickly learned to be quiet and restrained. But now, as an adult, there's no reason to remain unseen and unheard — yet no one told your subconscious mind.

Look at it this way: Our failures should be seen as stepping stones that bring us closer to our goal. Our failures give us tremendous feedback. Isn't it true that with each perceived failure we learn something of value? Failure is our way of learning and growing. In reality, there is no such thing as failure: It's just part of our education on the way to our inevitable success — if we look at it that way.

Your situation will not improve if you do nothing about it. Of course, this is obvious. But then why are so many people waiting for their big break, or to win the lottery, or for some other miracle? Most people live with the idea that everything will magically work out. And then comes disappointment.

Success isn't handed to us on a silver platter; we have to take action, we have to challenge our old beliefs, and we have to risk failure.

What do most people do when they need money? Some borrow, and get deeper in debt. Others tighten their belts and adapt their needs to their meager income. Instead of challenging themselves and their world to fulfill their dreams, most people limit their dreams to their perceptions of the world's constraints. They have a passive, wait-and-see attitude — let's see if this miracle happens. And, most often, it doesn't happen.

OUR LIVES REFLECT OUR BELIEFS — UNLIMITED SUCCESS COMES FROM AN UNLIMITED BELIEF SYSTEM

To improve your financial situation, to track down a job, to get a raise in your salary, to double your income, to become fit and healthy, you have to passionately want to improve your life. You have to take action, adopt precise measures, and change your attitude. This has to become a fixed objective. This overriding desire is mandatory to create the life you want. Determination and will are all the strength you need. Kazuo Inamori, CEO of

Kyocera International and author of A *Passion for Success*, puts it this way:

> An entrepreneur must first have a clear vision of what he or she wants. A mere dream of what you want is not adequate. Instead, cultivate a desire so strong and a vision so clear that they become part of your subconscious mind.

So many people honestly desire to improve their lives, but still fail in their attempts to become successful. The reason is that they have mistaken *wishing* for *wanting*. Wishful thinking is far more common than really wanting something. A wish is weak, changeable, and passive. It's not strong enough to overcome procrastination or other obstacles that may arise in the process of getting what you want. Really wanting something is a spur to action. It does not tolerate delays. It bypasses obstacles. It gives us wings to fly with.

One day a wise man was asked by a disciple what it took to obtain wisdom. The sage led the disciple to a river and plunged his head underwater. After a few seconds, his anxious follower began struggling, afraid he was going to drown. But

the teacher continued to hold his head underwater. The student struggled even harder. Finally,
the wise man let him go just before he would have
drowned and asked him, "When your head was
underwater, what did you want most?" "To
breathe," the frightened boy answered. "Well,
there you have it. That's exactly how much you
must want wisdom."

Life gives you what you sincerely want. "You will
become as great as your dominant aspiration,"
James Allen wrote in his classic work *As You Think*.
"If you cherish a vision, a lofty ideal in your heart,
you will realize it." If you content yourself with
mediocrity, that is what you will have. Since you
are reading this book, you're probably not completely satisfied with your situation. Something is
intensely motivating about dissatisfaction: Dissatisfaction fuels dreams. As we mentioned before,
many successful people had difficult, impoverished childhoods. They felt humiliated. Their
desire to rise above poverty and low social status
was so intense that it propelled them toward
their dreams. "Even with such strong desires, circumstances will change..." Inamori says. "Still, do
not use these circumstances as excuses. Your

determination should be so strong as to overcome any obstacles, foreseen or unforeseen."

The dreams you carry and nourish in your heart are your most noble part. Those who stop dreaming, those who ignore their most intense yearnings are living a life of emptiness and frustration. Don't let this happen to you. Change your life by daring to let yourself be carried away by your dreams and to live out your dreams to the fullest.

This philosophy may appear naive — it is. Without naivete, without the innocence of dreams, nothing great would have been created in this world. Humans would not fly; epic films would not have been made; Ford wouldn't have created the mass-produced automobile; Edison wouldn't have lit the world. A serious outlook, cynicism, and even strictly rational thought are great obstacles to success. We aren't arguing in favor of extravagant, irrational behavior. Far from it! The truth is: At the root of every great discovery and exceptional success story lies a dream, an aspiration, a desire. This desire transcends cynicism and strictly rational thought.

Within your deepest desires and highest dreams are the keys to your success.

SUMMARY AND RECOMMENDED ACTION

To sum up this first chapter, there are four initial conditions to fulfill in order to become successful:

1. *Believe you will be successful.* The first prerequisite is having faith, believing that you can attain success, believing in yourself. This belief can be created by using self-suggestion to change your old programming. If you don't believe in yourself or your ideas, you'll never convince anyone else to believe in them. Success never comes out of the blue, handed to you on a silver platter. The obstacles you'll have to overcome, the difficulties you'll inevitably meet, and the sustained effort you need to make all require a good dose of faith to spur you on.

2. *Be aware that your situation will not magically change if you do nothing about it.* In your current endeavors, and in your future plans, you could even establish the following behavioral principle: If you don't completely and honestly believe in what you're about to do, don't do it, otherwise you will probably fail. When you don't believe in something, the codes you program into your

subconscious and the messages you give to those who would help you are false, vague, and contradictory. Partial conviction leads to partial success, and that means partial failure. Doubt is reflected in poor results.

3. *Passionately desire to improve your life.* Make a list of the excuses and the inner monologues that keep success at bay. This stage is absolutely essential. It makes you aware of your limiting beliefs. Once you know them, you can overcome them. Successful people have learned to release doubt from their minds. They have tremendous faith in both themselves and in their plans, despite any opposition they may face.

4. *Dare to dream — and to dream great dreams. Within your deepest desires and highest dreams are the keys to success.* Your subconscious mind knows only those limitations you have imposed upon it through your own limiting beliefs — and those beliefs can be changed, using the tools in this book.

Chapter 2

—⁓—

Wealth Is a State of Mind

Mind is the master power that molds and makes,
And we are mind, and evermore we take
The tool of thought, and shaping what we will,
Bring forth a thousand joys, a thousand ills.
We think in secret, and it comes to pass,
Our world is but our looking glass.

— JAMES ALLEN, author of *As You Think*

THE MOST COMMON MISTAKE we make is looking outside of us for what we should find inside. Success is no exception. Just as the source of true happiness lies within each of us, success also comes from within. Success is the result of a very specific mental attitude. Call it what you like: the mentality of the rich, an attitude of success, prosperity consciousness. Success is the outward manifestation of an inner focus, the result of steering thoughts toward a specific target.

Unfortunately, most people are unaware of this. Most of the principles in the following chapters all lead to a higher, universal truth: *The mind is capable of anything.* Genuine wealth is, above all, a state of mind — a state that has taken form in the lives of the rich and successful. We have to begin by being rich in mind before we can become rich in life, successful in mind before we can be successful in life.

Gaining a clear understanding of the subconscious is fundamental. It's all very well to tell people that they must believe in success and fortune and want it passionately. Yet, most people are paralyzed by bad experiences. They appear completely incapable of cultivating what Friedrich Nietzsche called "the will to power." It's not at all easy to demand action and firmness from someone who is uncertain, indecisive, passive, and unmotivated. By discovering the mechanisms and power of the subconscious mind, however, anyone can overcome these obstacles.

Our Subconscious Mind Is Limitless

We are the creators of our own happiness or misery. Truly understanding this statement can be our most important motivator.

The key to success ultimately lies in the

proper use of the subconscious mind. Both the means to make money and the outside circumstances affecting us are so varied and so personal that it would be impossible to propose a single surefire winning formula to create success. No miracle recipe exists — but there is a common theme through all success stories. This single, simple theme is *a positive inner attitude*.

Analysis and research only go so far. And then our sixth sense, what some people call business sense or intuition, comes into play — the result of positive mental programming and a well-utilized subconscious mind. The subconscious mind is best represented by the image of the iceberg: The small, visible part is the conscious mind while the submerged and much larger part is the subconscious. The role of the subconscious in our lives is much greater than most of us understand. It's the seat of our habits, complexes, and the limitations of our personalities. No matter what we think, *the subconscious — not outside circumstances — is responsible for an individual's success or failure.*

There are many ways we train our subconscious. One of the strongest ways is through our beliefs. Peter Senge, author of *The Fifth Discipline*, writes:

> Most of us hold one of two contradictory beliefs that limit our ability to create what we really want. The more common is the belief in our *powerlessness* — our inability to bring into being all the things we really care about. The other belief centers on *unworthiness* — that we do not deserve to have what we truly want....
>
> There are many ways by which the subconscious gets programmed. Cultures program the subconscious. Beliefs program the subconscious. It is well established, for example, that beliefs affect perception: If you believe that people are untrustworthy, you will continually "see" double-dealing and chicanery that others without this belief would not see.

The subconscious can be compared to a computer. It blindly and infallibly executes the program fed into it. An appropriate phrase from the computer industry is GIGO — Garbage In, Garbage Out. Much of our programming from infancy onward has been negative garbage, coming straight from negative belief systems.

In early childhood, our critical sense is still undeveloped, and we naturally accept all suggestions from the outside world. The program's database, so to speak, comes at first from parents and teachers, media and peers. Their words become engraved in our young minds, which are as impressionable as soft clay. A single word can blight someone's life, or at least weigh them down for a long time. This word may have been said without malice, but if it contained fear and negativity, the effects can be disastrous. A pessimistic mother, one day snapping in frustration, may tell a child she considers too impulsive or whimsical, "Quit dreaming — stop living in the clouds. Who do you think you are?" These remarks are recorded in the child's subconscious and become part of their mental programming. The job of the subconscious, which has almost limitless power, is to execute this program, making the child fail over and over again. The most tragic thing of all is that people who have had this type of early conditioning can spend their entire lives unaware that they are the victims of negative mental programming.

Words are extremely powerful agents. A declaration of love, a piece of bad news, a word of congratulations all have a major impact on our inner state. And *the words don't even have to be true for the mind to accept them.*

Thomas Peters and Robert Waterman, authors of *In Search of Excellence*, describe an experiment that illustrates the power of words, even when those words are untrue:

> The old adage is "nothing succeeds like success." It turns out to have a sound scientific basis. Researchers studying motivation find that the prime factor is simply the self-perception among motivated subjects that they are, in fact, doing well. Whether they are or not by any absolute standard doesn't seem to matter much. In one experiment, adults were given ten puzzles to solve. All ten were exactly the same for all subjects. They worked on them, turned them in, and were given the results at the end. Now, in fact, the results they were given were fictitious. Half of the exam takers were told that they had done well, with seven out of ten

correct. The other half were told they had done poorly, with seven out of ten wrong. Then all were given another ten puzzles (the same for each person). The half who had been *told* that they had done well in the first round really did do better in the second, and the other half really did do worse. Mere association with past personal success apparently leads to more persistence, higher motivation, or something that makes us do better.

The result of this experiment is worth some thought. The subjects' subconscious minds were influenced by the falsified results. Perception alone radically improved one group's performance and weakened the other's.

A little further on, the same authors advance the following theory as a result of this experiment: "We often argue that the excellent companies are the way they are because they are organized to obtain extraordinary effort from ordinary human beings." What applies to businesses certainly applies equally to individuals. Their secret: a well-guided subconscious mind.

In addition to parents, teachers, and friends who clumsily express negativity without realizing the harmful impact they have, there is another very important programming agent as well: the individual. All of us have our own inner monologues that program us constantly. We repeat to ourselves: "Nothing ever works out for me." "I'm always tired." "What am I doing with my life?" "I'm not appreciated enough." "I'm not good enough." "It's so hard to succeed." "I never have enough time." "I've wasted so much time." The list is endless. These negative, pessimistic thoughts that we repeat to ourselves, more or less consciously, influence or reinforce the current program.

But they don't have to stay in our consciousness. When we reach adulthood, we can take responsibility for our own belief systems. No programming has to be permanent. Any negative programming can be turned around. How? Through the power of even a single affirmation that effectively counteracts that negative programming.

The Power of Affirmations, The Power of Self-suggestion

How can we acquire a mentality that will

produce favorable circumstances and attract success? There are a wide variety of methods available, all based on some form of self-suggestion. These methods have a number of different names — mental programming, positive thinking, affirmation, self-hypnosis, psycho-cybernetics, the Alpha method. All of these techniques have proven to be effective. Both authors of this book have experienced wonderful results by using a simple formula or affirmation developed by a famous French pharmacist, Emile Coué.

Coué's discovery was accidental. One day, one of his clients insisted on buying a drug for which he needed a prescription. He had no prescription, but still stubbornly demanded the drug. Coué thought up a trick: He recommended a product that he said was just as effective, but was actually only a sugar pill. The patient came back a few days later, completely cured and absolutely delighted with the results. What was later called the placebo effect had just been discovered.

What had happened to this patient? It was essentially the same phenomenon that had occurred in the experiment in *In Search of Excellence*, except that the magical effect of words, of

confidence, and of the subconscious had acted on
the physical rather than the intellectual level. This
patient was cured by his confidence in the pharmacist and in the medication, as well as by the mental
certainty that he was going to get well.

It didn't take Coué long to realize the significance of this experiment. If a word could cure an
ailment, what could it do to someone's personality?
In the next few years he developed an extremely
simple formula, one that involved no sugar pills —
simply words. It has been applied throughout the
world and has improved the lives of thousands
of individuals. The formula is actually a simple
self-suggestion. Since Coué couldn't stay at each
patient's bedside, or stay in contact with them, the
patients could cure themselves using the formula,
which consisted of these words: *Every day, in every
way, I am getting better and better.*

Coué advised people to repeat this formula
aloud in a monotone voice at least twenty times a
day. Countless variations have been conceived. We
can each concoct our own according to our needs
and personality. The effects are astounding. This
general formula, this simple affirmation, embraces

all aspects of our lives and has limitless possibilities.

The golden rule of self-suggestion is repetition, so this should be repeated daily — throughout
the day — to have the best effect. A relaxed state,
where the subconscious is most receptive to new
information, is the best — though not essential.
It makes the process effective much more quickly,
however. You are naturally in a relaxed state after
meditation, upon awakening, or at bedtime. Or it
can easily be self-induced: To do this, lie down or
seat yourself comfortably in an armchair, and close
your eyes. Inhale deeply several times. Then relax
each separate part of the body, beginning with the
feet, ankles, legs, and on up to the head.

You must literally flood your subconscious
with your new formula. Little by little, a new program will set in, and a new personality will emerge.
Negative reinforcement will give way to positive
reinforcement, to enthusiasm, energy, boldness,
and determination. Don't be put off by the simplicity of this method, like many of Emile Coué's
contemporaries, who refused to believe that such a
simple technique could be effective. We're living
proof this technique is effective! Try it, several

times a day for at least a month, and see the results for yourself.

Many successful people, when faced with adversity, have subconsciously resorted to this technique, or others like it. Whether confronted by problems or on the threshold of a new adventure, they learned to condition or reprogram themselves by repeating the ideas that they would reach success, that no obstacle would hinder their attempts, that their visions would certainly become reality.

The cumulative result of all our inner programming is our self-image. Despite our conscious efforts to create a self-image, each of us has only a vague idea of the one we actually project. We have an even more vague idea of the role self-image plays in our lives. It's important to understand this because people are what they believe themselves to be. Everything in our lives, including our wealth, joy, and physical shape, is directly proportional to our self-image, directly influenced by our self-image.

Senge adds another important point: "Ultimately, what matters most in developing the subconscious...is the genuine caring for the desired outcome, the deep feeling of it being the 'right' goal toward which to aspire. The subconscious seems especially receptive to goals in line with our deeper aspiration and values. According to some spiritual disciplines, this is because these deeper aspirations input directly to, or are part of, the subconscious mind."

His words are worth pondering.

PICTURE YOUR SUCCESS — IMAGINE IT CLEARLY

What do you want? What does your version of success look like? You are unique; you have a unique definition of success, and success can only come through your unique vision. Those who see themselves as nothing but lowly employees, who can't imagine ever being able to scale the corporate ladder, will stay in lowly positions. "There's no way I can double my income in a year!" If this is what we believe, life proves us right.

We always establish our goals according to our self-image. It's therefore just as hard for us to fail as to succeed. And it's just as easy for us to succeed as it is to fail. *A new self-image produces a new goal, and a new goal results in a new life.*

In her powerful book *Creative Visualization*, Shakti Gawain writes, "Creative visualization is the technique of using your imagination to create what you want in your life." All successful people pictured themselves successful before achieving their dreams. No matter how poor they were in the beginning, no matter how little education they had, no matter how few contacts they had, all of them pictured themselves successful. They became convinced they would be successful. Life answered their dreams in accordance with their self-image and the faith they had in their success.

Because of this direct correlation between your self-image and what life offers you, it's extremely worthwhile to work on your self-image, so that *every day in every way, you are getting better and better.* This affirmation does wonders for your self-image. You can change your self-image at any time, according to your aspirations.

In the beginning, when you begin reprogramming yourself and shaping a new self-image, you'll inevitably be influenced by your old image. This is completely natural. Change takes place in gradual stages. But you'll eventually develop a new self-image, and it will produce new goals — and new goals will, inevitably, change your life for the better.

Experience has shown that to be fully effective self-suggestions or affirmations should be: (1) *brief* — if they are too long, they will not be effective — and (2) *positive*, which is absolutely essential. The subconscious works differently from the conscious mind. If you say, "I'm not poor anymore," the word *poor* might be subconsciously retained because it is the key word. Repeating the statement with the negative word could produce the opposite results of what you want. We have to take a positive, yet gradual, approach. Some authors write that we must formulate our suggestions as if we already have what we desire: "I am now rich." This *could* be counterproductive in some cases, however, because our conscious mind might see a contradiction here. Mental conflict could arise to compromise the positive results of the suggestion. If you repeat, "I am now rich," or "My job is perfect," at least some part of your mind will naturally sense the inconsistency, especially if you're broke or out of work. In our opinion, it's better to say, "I'm getting more and more successful, day by day," or "I am creating a perfect job."

It's important to find the affirmation that feels positive and empowering for you.

Affirmations guarantee success. We know this from experience. Even starting with a mechanical and barely convincing repetition of your words has some effect. The more emotion and feeling you put into your suggestion, however, the better the results will be. Don't impose limitations on your affirmations. Your potential is extraordinary. As Ray Kroc, the founder of McDonald's, said, "Think big and you'll become big."

Summary and Recommended Action

To sum up this chapter, these are the ways to imprint powerful change in your life:

1. *Write down your version of success in the form of an affirmation that is particularly powerful for you.* An example might be, "I now have an annual income of $_____" or "I am creating the perfect job for myself." This simple act will have a great impact on you, giving your thoughts more power and authority. It becomes a springboard for change. Never lose sight of your affirmation — it is your formula for success. Leave it in a place where you will

see it regularly, and continue to affirm it regularly.

2. *Another way to imprint powerful change is to repeat single words frequently.* For example, many successful people share the following characteristics — they are:

- Persistent
- Enthusiastic
- Energetic
- Bold
- Intuitive
- Persuasive
- Authoritative
- Fun-loving

- Confident
- Imaginative
- Diligent
- Positive
- Astute
- Dependable
- Daring
- Relaxed

Pick a word that describes a characteristic you want to strengthen in yourself, and repeat the word throughout the day. Or affirm "I am _____." This is a very effective technique.

3. *Make a list of the qualities you would like to develop more fully, using or adding to the list above.* Choose the qualities you need to work on the most. Work on one at a time, starting with your weakest. Feel how much stronger you soon become.

4. *Affirm to yourself, repeatedly: Every day, in every way, I am getting better and better.*

Chapter 3

—ᴍᴍ—

Eliminating
Mental Blocks

*To succeed, we must have a desire so strong
that it reaches and permeates our subconscious minds.*

— KAZUO INAMORI, founder and chairman
of two of Japan's most successful companies
and author of *A Passion for Success*

PERHAPS THIS IS THE ONLY SINGLE piece of
advice you'll need to create the success you
want: *To succeed, we must have a desire so strong that it
permeates our subconscious minds.* Once this happens,
we connect with the infinite organizing power of
the universe, and it supports our desire. Once this
happens, we create what we want in life, and we
create a new self-image as well in the process.

Creating a new self-image inevitably entails
letting go of the old one. Yet everyone resists
this kind of change. Everyone has created mental
blocks that work to prevent change, even change
for the good.

Mental blocks are unconscious beliefs that have been reinforced by experiences in our lives. Willis Harmon discusses unconscious beliefs in his book *Global Mind Change:*

> A person's *total belief system* is an organization of beliefs and expectancies that the person accepts as true of the world he or she lives in — verbal and nonverbal, implicit and explicit, conscious and unconscious. The belief system does not have to be logically consistent; indeed, it probably never is.

One of the most common, deeply embedded, and harmful mental blocks is the belief that money is bad. This can often be traced to the Judeo-Christian Bible passage, "Money is the root of all evil." Actually, the entire passage reads, "The love of money is the root of all evil." Certainly, the *love* of money can promote greed and selfishness. The danger lies in becoming a slave to money — it is an excellent servant, but a cunning and powerful master. It can be seductive, drawing all one's time and energy into its acquisition. It's important to keep this in mind as you begin to make more of it — as you inevitably will if you continue reading books like this one and absorbing these principles of wealth, consciously and subconsciously. If we're honest with ourselves, we intuitively know whether our relationship with money is positive or not.

Money is badly maligned in many areas of our society, and some of the reasons are justified. But performing our service effectively — and being well rewarded for it — can be very positive, for ourselves and our world.

CREATE A POSITIVE VIEW OF MONEY — MONEY CAN BE A POWERFUL AGENT OF GOOD IN THE WORLD

Through our work we create ideas, innovative products, jobs, beautiful works of art, educational tools, and so on, endlessly. And those who truly understand real success give back to their communities and their world through philanthropy and many other forms of financial and visionary support. There are literally millions of wealthy people who are the opposite of the unscrupulous, mean-spirited money-grubber who seeks materialism for its own sake, for greedy acquisition and consumption. It's no coincidence that the richest countries in the world also have reached the highest achievements in culture and science. Money affords us the time and resources to pursue desires beyond basic human needs, to create things that are as important as survival itself.

Money is simply a recognition of services rendered. Most people who become wealthy have provided services to many people and have been justly rewarded for them. Walt Disney brightened the lives of millions of children, and adults as well. The list of contributions made by the wealthy is endless, for money is power — power to do a great deal of good in the world.

Henry Ford was once asked what he would do if he lost his entire fortune. Without a moment's hesitation, he said he would think up another fundamental human need and meet it by offering a cheaper and more efficient service than anybody else. He said that he would be a millionaire again within five years.

Many people have an aversion to money. This aversion is often hypocritical: People malign the rich but secretly envy them. Once you begin to understand some of the principles in this book and begin providing the kind of services to humanity that will make you substantial amounts of money, your attitude toward the rich will change completely — because you'll become one of them. And you'll be able to do a lot of good for a lot of people with your wealth.

Another prevalent mental block is the fear of going against family background and upbringing — outdoing one's parents, for example. Not everyone suffers from this, of course; we have already seen that poverty can be a strong catalyst for success. But in many cases poverty is a form of neurotic behavior — a mental rut that goes nowhere, the reflection of an impoverished self-image. Mental blocks around the issue of making money come disguised in a great variety of forms that we need to examine as we recognize them in ourselves.

It's important to integrate a positive view of money and success into your new self-image. Be vigilant and honest with yourself; identify your mental blocks and release them. Identify your limiting beliefs and change them. Replace them with more positive, powerful thoughts. *Both poverty and riches are the offspring of thought.*

There Are No Limitations
to the Mind

This is a very powerful truth, one that bears repeating: *There are no limitations to the mind except those we accept.* Once we understand this as a truth, we can become successful and shape our present and future life to match our aspirations. When we apply this truth to our lives, our circumstances become whatever we desire; our lives become whatever we want them to be.

If you steer your thoughts in a positive, expansive direction, you'll become as powerful as you can imagine. Every day, make sure that you devote some time to reprogramming yourself, to creative visualization, guided imagery, daydreaming. Many people are paid extraordinary salaries to daydream! Our most lucrative thoughts can come through daydreaming, free-rambling fantasy, and brainstorming future possibilities.

Daydreams are often maligned by "down-to-earth" people who say that we have to look life squarely in the face and accept our fate, even if it leaves a lot to be desired. Yet, these resigned and unhappy individuals forget that there are two types of dreamers: those who make no attempt to turn their dreams into reality, and those who understand and believe in the creative power of the subconscious. These are the dreamers who take concrete measures to fulfill their dreams. These are the dreamers who shape our world, and who create wealth for themselves and others in the process.

In *The Seven Spiritual Laws of Success*, Deepak Chopra says:

> Inherent in every intention and desire is the seed and mechanics for its fulfillment. Intention and desire in the field of pure potentiality have infinite organizing power. And when we introduce an intention in the fertile ground of pure potentiality, we put this infinite organizing power to work for us.

Let's examine what Chopra is saying. If intention is thought and our thoughts are filled with negative ideas toward money (we can only make enough to get by, for example, or there is never enough), we will fulfill these thoughts. If, however, we fill our mind with new and positive images (there are no limits, as the universe contains infinite possibilities), we will fulfill these thoughts, and become as successful as we can possibly imagine.

Clearly imagine that you already have what you hope for, that you have reached your goals. What does your life look like? One reason this exercise of imagination is so effective is that the subconscious is not governed by the same rules of time as the conscious mind. In fact, time doesn't exist in the subconscious mind — or in our dreams, which are the subconscious mind's most easily recognizable by-product.

This is why trauma experienced in early childhood can affect people long after they are an adult; rational minds understand that they no longer have to worry about the past, but the subconscious may not recognize the difference. This is also why we can pretend that something is true in our fantasies and our visualizations, and the subconscious mind will go about its work and bring what we imagine into reality, whether the things we imagine are our fears or our ardent desires for the very best.

This may seem to contradict what we said

earlier (on page 57) about affirmations. In our fantasies and visualizations, however, it is very effective to imagine as fully as possible that we have created the future we dream of.

OUR THOUGHTS MATERIALIZE

All of our thoughts tend to materialize in our lives, when they are repeated enough. This is why, in order to succeed, we have to monitor our thoughts closely. If we continually focus on financial troubles, we invite them to stay. *Wherever you focus your attention, wherever you put your energy, that is what will grow.* If you focus on the good that you want, you welcome abundance, prosperity, and success. If you focus on how little money you bring home every month, you will continue to experience frustration and need. However, if you focus on putting even a small amount away — just ten dollars a week in a savings account, for example — and imagine the account growing, you will begin to create abundance in your life because your focus will shift from "lack of" to "growth." Try it, and you'll be amazed at how different it feels to focus on growth rather than lack, on prosperity rather than poverty. The subconscious is a vast field, governed by the universal law of cause and effect. As we sow, so we reap. Thoughts and ideas are the cause; facts and events are the effect.

Most people have more imagination for conjuring up problems that prevent them from realizing their dreams than for recognizing their opportunities for success. Stephen Covey, author of *The Seven Habits of Highly Effective People*, emphasizes this point:

> Habits have tremendous gravity pull. Like any natural force, gravity pull can work with us or against us. The gravity pull of some of our habits may currently be keeping us from going where we want to go. Breaking deeply imbedded habitual tendencies such as procrastination, impatience, criticalness, or selfishness that violate basic principles of human effectiveness involves more than a little willpower and a few minor changes in our lives. It takes tremendous effort to break free from the gravity pull of such habits, but once we do, our freedom takes on a whole new dimension.

Change — real change — comes from the inside out.... It comes from striking at the root — the fabric of our thought, the fundamental, essential paradigms, which give definition to our character and create the lens through which we see the world.

Successful people are inspired by their dreams, and they focus on the means to reach them, not on what's keeping them from realizing them. Inventors see their inventions. Artists see their completed works. Successful entrepreneurs see their businesses thriving. Visionaries, social workers, nonprofit workers, even some politicians see society changed for the better.

Ted Turner, creator of a broadcast empire, says: "A visionary is supposed to have a vision of the future." Ideas govern the world. The power they have is phenomenal. It is therefore necessary to *repeatedly* fill our minds with thoughts of service, abundance, and success — to break free of the gravity pull of our negative thoughts. Eventually, we replace the old, negative thoughts with a new, positive self-image. Each thought has energy and, through some mysterious law of attraction, draws objects, beings, and circumstances of a similar nature to it — like a magnet. Negative thoughts attract negative experiences. Positive thoughts attract positive experiences.

Unfortunately, this truth is not always supported by society. Our educational system generally supports and encourages the rational and strictly logical part of thought, while neglecting or even scorning its intuitive and imaginative side. The right side of the brain is too often ignored.

And yet, nothing great has ever been achieved without an original dream. A dream is a kind of projection of our inner selves. What, in fact, is a projection or a project? By definition, it's a part of ourselves that we throw forward. The greater we program our self-images to be, the more grandiose our dreams will be. And our dreams, however bold they may be, are often more easily attainable than we might even believe at the moment.

Steven Spielberg once dreamed of making a certain film. He had the script, but he needed a producer to finance it. One day, while walking on the beach, he "accidentally" met a rich man who was ready to invest in young filmmakers. With the money Spielberg received from this producer, a total stranger to him at the time, he was able to shoot *Amblin,* which was given an Honorable Mention at the Venice Film Festival and drew attention to him in Hollywood.

This is often how the subconscious solves a problem: We have a chance encounter, or we happen to see an article or TV show that provides a clear-cut answer to a dilemma, or our family or friends somehow contribute to our success — sometimes in ways they aren't even aware of at the time.

When others point to fate, or to difficult circumstances, believing we need to be "resigned to our fate," we point out that the world is governed mentally and physically by cause and effect, and so we create our fate; it's the result of our thoughts and actions. The same is true for good and bad luck: They're the consequences of our thoughts and actions. We literally make our own good and bad luck. This is why people who correctly learn and apply the laws of the mind and success forge their own destiny.

The supreme secret of success is a secret not because anyone is trying to keep it secret, but only because so few understand it. This secret can be told in a few simple words, and success will come to you when you truly understand these words: *The human mind can accomplish whatever it believes in.*

Here's another way to sum it up: *If you think you can, or if you think you can't, you're right.*

Summary and Recommended Action

To integrate a positive view of money and success in your life:

1. *Identify your mental blocks about money and success.* Explore your relationship with money — is it positive or negative? As you become aware of your thoughts in relation to money, write them down. Take a look at why you might have particular thoughts or beliefs. Then release any old ways of thinking that aren't supportive of your greatest dreams.

2. *Monitor your thoughts closely.* Focus on the good you want. Welcome abundance, prosperity, and success into your life. Perhaps you'll want to open a bank account, and start by putting a small amount each week into it. Whenever your thoughts are focused on how little you have, make a conscious effort to think about your new account and

its inevitable growth over the years, as you continue to add to it. You'll start to feel the difference between focusing on "growth and abundance" and focusing on "lack." Eventually your focus will shift without conscious effort. All your thoughts can be shifted this way.

3. *Reprogram your thoughts.* Do some of the exercises in this book. Every day, make sure that you devote some time to reprogramming yourself, to creative visualization, guided imagery, and daydreaming. In a relaxed state, fill your mind with new and positive images. Fantasize that you have already achieved the greatest success you can imagine. Visualize and feel what it's like to already have reached your goals. Do so *repeatedly*, day after day, week after week. You'll soon see some exciting changes happening in your life.

Chapter 4

—∿—

Making Decisions

One of our greatest gifts is our intuition. It's a sixth sense we all have — we just need to learn to access it, to tap into it, and to trust it.

— DONNA KARAN, designer and chief executive officer of the international fashion empire DKNY

HAVING A DREAM, and having confidence in yourself, is one thing — but how do you know whether your dream is a good idea, and you're not making a disastrous mistake? We are constantly called upon to make decisions, whether to look for a new job, choose a career, back a project, or make an investment.

A wrong move in business or your career, while certainly not fatal, can mean a substantial setback. We have to learn how to make right decisions more often than wrong ones. It's encouraging to note that most successful people don't believe that this ability is inborn, but that it can be acquired and enhanced. This ability is accessible to anyone who takes the time and energy to cultivate it.

Some plans are simply not viable. Mark McCormack, author of *What They Don't Teach You at Harvard Business School,* supplies an amusing example of this principle:

> A dog-food company was holding its annual sales convention. During the course of the convention the president of the company listened patiently as his advertising director introduced a point-of-sale scheme that would "revolutionize the industry," and his sales director extolled the virtues of the "best damn sales force in the business." Finally it was time for the president to go to the podium and make his closing remarks.
>
> "Over the past few days," he began, "we've heard from all our division heads of their wonderful plans for the coming year. Now as we draw to a close, I have only one question. If we have the best advertising, the best marketing, the best sales force, how come we sell less damn dog food than anyone in the business?"

Absolute silence filled the convention hall. Finally, after what seemed like forever, a small voice answered from the back of the room: "Because the dogs *hate* it."

The best marketing in the world won't help an inferior product, or a service that doesn't fill a need. How do we know if our plan is viable or not? We've got to learn to access, tap into, and trust our intuition.

While the Wright brothers were inventing their plane, scientific studies were undertaken to demonstrate that a body heavier than air could not possibly fly. And Ray Kroc's friends thought entering the business of selling cheap hamburgers was sheer lunacy. We need to enhance our capacity to see possibilities where others see only difficulties, or even impossibilities. Sam Walton, founder and chairman of Wal-Mart, explains in his book *Made in America* how recognizing opportunity out of necessity helped him make his company the phenomenal success that it is today:

Many of our best opportunities were created out of necessity. The things that we were forced to do, because we started

out underfinanced and undercapitalized
in remote, small communities, contributed
mightily to the way we've grown as a company.

Because Walton had the capacity to see possibilities where others saw only difficulties or impossibilities, his company grew and continues to grow
and flourish.

This is another key to success, and it's worth
giving some thought.

Look for Possibilities
Where Others See Only Difficulties

One day, over fifty years ago, a man was
taking a photograph of his young daughter, and she
asked him why they had to wait to see the pictures.
This naive question intrigued her father, inventor
Edwin H. Land. All of Land's scientist friends told
him his dream was impossible and his plan a waste
of time and money. In November 1948, the first 60-
second Polaroid camera went on sale in Boston,
and it caused a stampede of customers.

How often have you seen people raise their

eyebrows at one of your seemingly impossible schemes? How often have you judged something unlikely or impossible to achieve before realizing that just the opposite was true? Because of "rational reasons," or, more often, a secret lack of confidence, we give up our dreams, and console ourselves with the thought that it wouldn't have worked out anyway. This problem is directly linked with our self-image. The better our self-image, the more likely we'll be able to see that a range of possibilities exists, and the more likely we'll take the risk necessary to act on the opportunities we see.

Many unrealized plans and ideas are initially neither feasible nor unfeasible. What determines success or failure when putting them into action is the quantity and quality of the energy invested. They come to life and become viable through the sheer force of the vitality and energy put into them. People with positive, healthy self-images are powerhouses of energy and can easily tap into the unlimited reserves of their subconscious mind. They can create dog food that dogs love.

One flaw in many people who hesitate in

carrying out a plan is that they try to identify all the potential obstacles they might face, and they ignore the tools they have at their disposal to combat those problems — a paralyzing, anxiety-producing attitude if ever there was one! A far more skillful and effective approach is to focus on all the reasons you're likely to succeed instead of conjuring up all the possible stumbling blocks. We must, of course, weigh pros and cons. What happens in many cases, however, is despite ten favorable reasons, one negative reason discourages most people from trying at all. This comes from our negative programming, which, through the principle of attraction, provides fertile ground for a single obstacle to thrive. Focusing on the negative can distort our judgment and paralyze our actions.

Naturally, it's extremely important to learn as much as possible beforehand about a proposed plan, job offer, or business deal. But there are always imponderables. Even the most detailed and sophisticated analysis will never completely dispel the unknown. Studies undertaken by corporations and individuals alike often confirm their original ideas. Facts can't take the place of intuition. We must discover how to interpret facts and draw our own conclusions from the data, using our intuition to guide us.

TRUST YOUR INTUITION

The ability to trust and rely on your sixth sense — your intuition — is the cornerstone of success. This sense can be developed so that it becomes second nature and enables you to make faster and more reliable decisions. If a plan is intuitively right for you, it excites you, it "feels good." If your plan doesn't fire you up, it's best to discard it for another — one that you believe in, one that excites you.

It's time to reeducate your intellect to recognize your intuition as a valid source of information and guidance. You can train your intellect to listen to and express your intuitive voice. The intellect is by nature very disciplined. This discipline can help you to ask for and receive the direction of your intuitive self.

How do you know when to make a decision? How do you know whether you have examined the situation enough and have all the necessary facts at your disposal? The answer is to rely on your subconscious program by repeating, "The right answer will come to me, easily and effortlessly." Or, "My inner guidance is giving me the right answer." Or, "My inner powers allow me to make the right decision." Find the words that feel best to you. With these kinds of affirmations, you are literally calling forth the wisdom of your intuitive mind.

Shakti Gawain, in *Living in the Light,* outlines a simple method of learning to trust your intuition:

> What does it mean to trust your intuition?... It means tuning in to your "gut feelings" about things — that deepest inner sense of personal truth — in any given situation, and acting on them, moment by moment. Sometimes these "gut messages" may tell you to do something unexpected or inconsistent with your previous plans; they may require that you trust a hunch that seems illogical; you may feel more emotionally vulnerable than you are used to; you may express thoughts, feelings, or opinions foreign to your usual beliefs; perhaps follow a dream or fantasy; or take some degree of financial risk to do something that feels important to you....

How do you do it?... Learning to trust your intuition is an art form, and like all other art forms, it takes practice to perfect. Your intuition is always 100 percent correct, but it takes time to learn to *hear* it correctly.

It is often hard to distinguish the "voice" of our intuition from the many other "voices" that speak to us from within: the voice of our conscience, voices of our old programming and beliefs, other people's opinions, fears and doubts, rational head trips, and "good ideas."

Unfortunately, there is no surefire way to differentiate the true voice or feelings of your intuition from all the other voices. The first step is to pay attention to what you feel inside, to the inner dialogue that goes on within you. For example, you might feel, "I'd like to give Jim a call." Immediately, the doubting voice inside says, "Why call him at this time of day? He probably won't be home," and you automatically ignore your original impulse to call. What if you had called him? What if you had found him at home, and discovered he had something important to say to you?

As you become aware of the subtle inner dialogue between your intuition and your other inner voices, it's very important not to put yourself down or diminish the experience. Try to remain an objective observer. Notice what happens when you follow your intuitive feelings. The result is usually increased energy and power, and a sense of things flowing. Now, notice what happens when you doubt, suppress, or go against your feelings. Invariably, you will observe decreased energy, powerless or helpless feelings, and emotional and/or physical pain.

Here's another effective method to use when faced with a decision to make: Toss a coin. You might think we're joking, but we're not: Flipping a coin is a time-honored little trick that can help you contact your subconscious mind. Decide what each side represents, and then flip a coin. Watch your reactions. If it lands on heads, telling you to go ahead with your plan, and you're disappointed, it's probably because you don't really believe in it or wish to pursue it. If tails appears, and you are disappointed, then maybe you should forge ahead. But if you're happy with the outcome, you have your answer. The idea is not to consider the results as definite, but to use them as a means of helping with the decision — helping you see intuitively which side you really favor.

As you learn to live from your intuition, you give up making decisions with your head. You act moment by moment on what you feel, and allow things to unfold as you go. In this way, you are led in the right direction. Decisions are made easily and naturally.

If you're having difficulty making a decision, take a break. The break could last a minute, an hour, or a day or more. Allow time to review the facts, then set a deadline: "At 3:00 P.M. I will tell the Board my decision." The time frame will activate your intuitive decision-making process.

Another time-honored solution is to sleep on the problem. "Sleep is the mother of counsel." This old adage is true because we easily contact our subconscious at night. So many problems that seemed so intractable in the evening simply dissolve overnight; the morning light brings clarity, and the solution seems obvious.

Another invaluable technique, when faced with a problem or idea or opportunity, is to list all the pros and cons. This might seem obvious, but it's effective. If the scale tips in favor of one side right away, your decision is easy. If the pros and cons balance out, let your subconscious deal with it. It will find the right answer.

One point: If the pros and cons balance out evenly, this can indicate that the plan will run up against problems. Doubt can eventually undermine your enthusiasm and your belief in yourself. If you only half-believe in a project, the results will match the expectations.

THE IDEAL TIME IS NOW

Most people make the mistake of waiting for the ideal time. This is just another excuse. The ideal time to start succeeding is today, this very minute. Write down a plan of what you want to achieve, make that phone call you've been thinking of, or write that letter you've been intending to write. Do it now.

The fundamental weakness that ruins so many people's lives is procrastination. Time is a vital component of any dream. An idea that might be a brilliant success today might completely fail in a year. A phone call might work wonders at one moment and come to absolutely nothing at all at another. The best decision, almost always, is to *do it now.*

All successful people have developed the ability to make decisions and act quickly on those decisions. "Haste hinders good counsel" — so the proverb goes. Yet procrastination and slowness surely do more wrong than hasty decisions.

STICK TO YOUR DECISION

Another characteristic of successful people is that they stick to their decisions, regardless of circumstances, past failures, temporary setbacks, or others' opinions.

Sticking to your final decision confirms your inner certainty that you have aimed correctly. Those who constantly change their minds will never be successful. Vacillation is a sign of a mental state dominated by doubt. Since you have seen that circumstances reflect your inner thoughts, there can be no question that doubt leads straight to failure. Consequently, success depends on two vital factors: (1) Making clear decisions, and (2) sticking to them while jumping straight into action.

You need to stick to your decisions, yet you also need to know when to let them go. This is not a contradiction. In both cases, when you rely on your intuition, you'll receive the guidance you need. Even the most astute entrepreneurs have made decisions that took them to places they didn't anticipate. It's vital, therefore, not to be overly rigid. One key to success is finding the delicate balance between persistence and flexibility.

Don't Give Up Too Quickly

Most people fail because they give up *much* too quickly. They throw in the towel after one or two failures. Pride or a lack of self-confidence makes people give up too quickly. Colonel Sanders tried dozens of different times to sell his chicken before he finally succeeded. An engineer at Head, a sporting goods company, performed forty-three tests before he successfully developed a metal ski. If he had given up after a dozen attempts, or even forty-two attempts, someone else would have invented it.

All great success stories are punctuated with failures. Positive people don't let themselves be beaten down by their first blunders. And we all make blunders at first, until we figure out what works.

Many successful people look at it in a way that recognizes a somewhat mysterious phenomenon: Life seems to have been designed as some sort of test. When people show they can overcome obstacles and failures with unswerving persistence and faith, life seems to lay down its weapons of opposition, and fame and fortune appear, as if charmed by their vision and strength. Success often follows a resounding failure, as if life wants to reward the brave soul able to surmount such a devastating setback.

The most successful people, almost without exception, all failed — often more than once — before they were successful. But they didn't give up. They tried and tried again.

LEARN FROM PAST MISTAKES

There is no shame in making a mistake — though it's generally a waste of time and energy to make the same mistake twice. If we thoughtfully examine why we failed, we gain a clearer understanding of how to succeed. In this way, each failure leads us closer to success.

Determination, a quality absent in most people, is almost always generously rewarded. It must not, however, be confused with blind pigheadedness. To adapt quickly is one of the keys to success; so is pragmatic trial and error. Rely on your intuition, take action, and keep going.

Sochiro Honda, chairman of Honda, makes an important point:

> When days become this dark and gloomy, it means that the treasure I am looking for is about to be discovered. The great flash of light and hope that bursts forth makes me instantly forget my long hours of tedious work.

Once we achieve success, we see that all our past mistakes were an essential part of our ongoing education. We never regret the past: Every failure we created has served us well, for our success is built on the understanding we gained from all our past mistakes and missteps.

SUMMARY AND RECOMMENDED ACTION

1. *What do you want?* State it simply, and present a clear request to your subconscious mind. Write it out. Repeat it to yourself, preferably at night before going to bed. Your subconscious will demonstrate its limitless power, and guide you to the people, places, and circumstances that will lead you to fulfillment of your dreams.

2. *Look for possibilities where others see only difficulties or impossibilities.* Look for the opportunity within every adversity. If you believe that every time a difficult situation occurs you're being shown something, and you're learning something, you will make rapid progress on your journey to success.

3. *Remember to trust your intuition.* An important step in learning to hear and follow your intuition is simply to practice "checking in" regularly — at least twice a day. Take a moment or two to relax and tune into your gut feelings. Ask for help and guidance when you need it, and listen for answers, which may come in many forms: words, images, or feelings, from within you, or from your world.

Chapter 5

Do What You Love

*I believe if you have talent and skill,
you should spin off on your own
and become captain of your own destiny.*

— GEORGE LUCAS, founder
and chairman of Lucas Arts

66 **I** WOULD LOVE TO SET UP MY OWN BUSINESS, but I don't have the ability or financing."

"My dream was to become an actor, but my parents laughed at the idea. I work for the government instead."

"My job bores me to tears, but there's so much unemployment and downsizing going on that I'd better not kid myself about finding a better one."

"I used to dream of being a lawyer, but it would take years."

How often have we heard words like these, or variations on the same themes? How often have you had similar thoughts? Out of every ten people, how many can boast of really enjoying their jobs? Unfortunately, most people simply don't like what they do for a living. They're convinced that they're stuck in their drudgery, that they will never be able to change their situations. Fate, in other words, has permanently sentenced them to a life of mediocrity.

If you dislike your job, consider the following: You could die without having done what you really want to do. Aren't you worth more than that?

Take a typical day in the life of so many people: They work eight hours at a job they don't particularly enjoy, then sleep eight hours. This leaves them with eight hours they typically use to recover and to try to forget the frustrations heaped on them during the day. Their dissatisfaction affects their relationships with their spouses, children, and friends. And yet, they continue, *believing they must*.

Most people unwillingly drag themselves to work on Monday morning and watch the clock until Friday afternoon, when they can finally throw off the shackles they had to endure for five long, painful days. They only really live for two out of seven days, with Saturday generally spent winding down or getting life's necessities together, and Sunday already haunted by the gloomy specter of Monday-morning blues. And they tolerate this, year after year.

This passive, fatalistic view of life can be changed. Nothing obliges you to keep working at a job you don't like. You can do something about it. An inspiring job exists to fulfill everyone's passion. And you could start it right now. Is life so poorly designed that it's meant to frustrate us constantly and deprive us of what we truly want? Life isn't that cruel. At least, it doesn't have to be. *It's your choice.*

LIFE GIVES US EXACTLY WHAT WE EXPECT

The belief that dreams are impossible to achieve prevents most people from getting what they want. Their experience certainly seems to support this belief. They get exactly what they expect from life: boredom, frustration, obstacles, and small incomes. People are what they believe themselves to be, no more, no less.

Denying your personal inclinations and ambitions normally begins very early in life. Yet, to be happy and fulfilled, we have to be courageous enough to be ourselves, to discover what we want, and to go after it. We have to stop denying ourselves because of fear, doubt, or conformity to some "normal" behavior or way of life. It's a fallacy that we have to do unfulfilling things to earn a living.

In fact, to be successful, you have to first do what you enjoy in life. If you don't enjoy your work, you can't do it well. This is an absolute principle. When your heart isn't in something, you experience a drastic slump in energy and motivation. You inevitably come up with mediocre results, or at least with a much poorer performance than you would if you loved what you were doing. It then follows that your boss, associates, clients, or customers can't be completely satisfied with what you have accomplished.

As an unhappy employee, chances are slim that you will get promoted to a more interesting position or receive a substantial raise. As an unhappy business owner, chances are small that your business will flourish. Since you rarely work alone, your unhappiness can drag your colleagues down. The monetary rewards you get will reflect this.

And with poor monetary compensation, your motivation and the quality of your work plummets — another vicious cycle!

Mark McCormack, author of *What They Don't Teach You at Harvard Business School,* makes this excellent point:

> Boredom occurs when the learning curve flattens out. It can happen to anyone at any level of the corporation. In fact, it occurs most often in successful people who need more challenge and stimulation than do others. If you're bored it's your fault. You just aren't working hard enough at making your job interesting. It is also probably the reason you haven't been offered anything better. Find out what you love to do and you will be successful at it.

DO WHAT YOU LOVE

When we say — emphatically — that you must love your work, we are in no way suggesting that an ideal job will be devoid of frustration, disappointment, and problems. Every successful person has faced periods of discouragement, frustration, and even self-doubt. Your dream job will not be heaven on earth every day. It's more like true love: The deep bonds that bring and keep two people together allow them to overcome the dilemmas and obstacles that appear along the way. Thomas Watson, founder of IBM, said it this way: "Make room in your heart for work and put some heart into your work."

Successful people are ruled by passion and their hearts. They are romantics, whether in art or in the world of business. They are spurred into action by their love of their work and their desire to do new things, to take up new challenges, to face new risks. They carry their dreams in their hearts — and they do everything they can to achieve them.

PASSION AND POWER

In *Work with Passion*, author Nancy Anderson defines passion:

Passion is intense emotional excitement. It is a feeling that comes to those who feel intensely about some object, person, ideal, or belief. Human passions are released to create both good and evil. There are many examples in history that show the difference one passionate person can make. Every love story, every major change in history — social, economic, philosophical, and artistic — came about because of the participation of *passionate* individuals.

We all have the capacity to feel intense emotional excitement. However, few of us *act* on our passions. We bury our passion because, among other reasons, we were ridiculed early in life because our enthusiasm was not backed up with expertise. As soon as you give yourself permission to feel whatever you feel, that power will resurface, surprising all who "knew you when." Then you will take action on those feelings.

Power is *the ability to take action.* As an adult, you know that your decisions are your choices. It is no longer necessary to do anything you hate — you can choose to do only what you truly love to do. That is power. That is passion in action.

Here's a good question to ask yourself: If you won ten million dollars, would you stay in your present job? If your answer is "Yes," congratulations! If not, then creating a situation in which you would answer "yes" to that question could be a very important goal. Here are a few principles to move you toward this goal:

- The only way to be happy and successful is to do what you truly enjoy doing. There is an ideal job or career for each one of us, a service that we can provide that no one else can do in quite the same way.

- You can do whatever you like, provided you put the necessary energy and determination into it.

- You alone can shape your destiny and decide to do what you enjoy, regardless of obstacles. The greatest barrier to success is yourself.

- Dare to do what you love. Overcome your fear-based mental and emotional blocks and you will succeed.

William O'Brian of Hanover Insurance puts it this way in an interview with Peter Senge in *The Fifth Discipline:* "To seek personal fulfillment only outside of work and to ignore the significant portion of our lives that we spend working would be to limit our opportunities to be happy and complete human beings."

BECOME THE BEST AT WHAT YOU DO

In his autobiography, Henry Ford said, "I determined resolutely that I would never join a company in which finance came before the work." For Ford, "the only foundation of real business is service."

Success is built on service. Successful service is built on one attitude: the attitude of doing the best we can, working to be the best in our field. Many successful people are motivated into action by the need to do things well and to accomplish something that will help other people. Making a profit is not their primary purpose, yet they usually make far more money than those who work primarily for profit. Steve Jobs, founder of Apple Computer, has said, "We're doing this because we really care about the higher educational process, not because we want to make a buck."

Wealth is the reward we receive in exchange for services we render. If we give the best service, then we can expect a commensurate reward. It is very powerful, then, to program our subconscious toward becoming the best in our field in a given period of time. As we give ourselves completely to our gift — our service — our gift gives back to us abundantly.

Become an Expert in Your Chosen Field

While you don't necessarily have to pursue years of formal education, it's invaluable to pursue all avenues to becoming an expert in your field. In the world today, when last month's computer system is already out of date, you have to keep up with change. One of the fundamentals of success is having in-depth knowledge or specialization in your work. A lack of knowledge is one of the major roadblocks to success.

Start by considering the products or services you have to offer to the public before looking for profits. With a good product or service, money comes naturally. When you become the best in your field, and focus on serving, the money will follow. This is an ancient law that never fails.

BE AN ORIGINAL

Formal education is certainly not sufficient to guarantee success. Something more is needed — a spark of originality or boldness, which schools often fail to teach and sometimes stifle altogether. All too often, schools level out the thinking process and suppress the creativity that allows you to see new possibilities and original solutions.

Education, and society in general, too often nip personal aspirations in the bud. This insidious process begins early in life. Our fears of being different and our need to conform support the part of our subconscious programming that limits our dreams, ideas, and aspirations.

We all naturally imitate those around us, especially when we're young. Unfortunately, the vast majority of people have imitated passionless jobs, financial struggle, and mediocrity.

A small, inner voice nevertheless survives within each of us. Timid and worried, it whispers to us that our public images are false, that our genuine personalities are hidden and unexpressed. Frustration, sadness, and, in some cases, a dead feeling inside are some of the burdens we heap upon ourselves when we deny who we are and what we have to offer.

If we want to succeed, we have to be different. We have to fully be ourselves and not be afraid to assert our true personalities. We are unique individuals with a unique purpose in life. Each of us is an original.

MAKE YOUR DESIRES INTO INTENTIONS, AND MAKE THEM CRYSTAL CLEAR

"I don't have the faintest idea what I really want to do...." Sound familiar? This is an all-too-common complaint. So many people are overwhelmed with confusion, and yet they never sit down and ask themselves the simplest questions — the kind of questions we ask throughout this book. The answers to these questions would dissolve their confusion in an instant. When people complain about not knowing what they want to do with their lives, it's obvious they have spent years stifling their aspirations and ignoring their inner selves. By conforming to other people's expectations and ways of life, they have forgotten who they are and have sowed the seeds of their confusion.

Anyone who doesn't really know what he or she wants to do and doesn't establish clear-cut goals will find it hard to succeed. The opposite is also true: *When we know perfectly well what we want to do in life, when our desire is crystal clear, the conditions enabling us to achieve it soon appear.* Often, extremely precise desires are fulfilled almost immediately.

A perfectly straightforward desire — devoid of hesitation, ambiguity, and contradiction — is very rare indeed. Vague, confused ambitions create a muddled subconscious. Since our aspirations are unclear, the results will be nebulous. A metamorphosis has to take place *within* — we have to form a clear picture of our ambitions and desires. We have to sculpt them to be clear and precise.

Don't underestimate the importance of this inner change. Until we are sure what we want, we won't get it. All successful people have unmistakable, clear ambitions and intentions. Their career choices were spawned by a deep sense of intuition that left no room for doubt. One of the most powerful keys to success, therefore, is knowing exactly what you want to be, do, and have.

Deepak Chopra's words are worth repeating again here: "Inherent in every intention and desire is the seed and mechanics for its fulfillment." In *The Seven Spiritual Laws of Success*, Chopra illuminates intention and desire in more detail, and adds another very important element of true, lasting success: *detachment.*

> Intention lays the groundwork for the effortless, spontaneous, frictionless flow of pure potentiality seeking expression from the unmanifest to the manifest....
> Intention is the real power behind desire. Intent alone is very powerful, because intent is desire without attachment to the outcome. Desire alone is weak, because desire in most people is intention with attachment.... Intention combined with detachment leads to life-centered, present-moment awareness. And when action is performed in present-moment awareness, it is most effective. Your *intent* is for the future, but your *attention* is in the present. As long as your attention is in the present,

then your intent for the future will manifest, because the future is created in the
present. Accept the present and intend the
future. The future is something you can
always create through detached intention.

Turn your wishes into crystal-clear *desires*.
Turn your desires into *intentions*. Once you intend
to do something, ninety percent of your perceived
obstacles vanish — and you have the tools to overcome the remaining ten percent. Such is the power
of your intent!

When you make an absolutely clear intention
to do something, and yet are not attached to the
results, you have an infallible formula for success
and fulfillment.

SUMMARY AND RECOMMENDED ACTION

To integrate passion and power in your work
life and to become the best at what you do:

1. *Think about your life as it is; then picture how
you want it to be.* If you're not doing what you like,
make a list of all of the reasons you can think of
that support your belief that you can't do what truly
excites and pleases you. Now go over the list point

by point and think about each reason. Are these obstacles really valid? If you can understand the principles in this book, you will understand that every obstacle can be overcome and turned into an opportunity. *If you think you can, or if you think you can't, you're right.*

2. *Ask yourself, if you had all the time and money in the world, what would you do?* If you would still do what you currently do, then you are on the right track, because you are passionate about what you do. If you would rather be doing something else, ask yourself: In what ways can I do the things I want now? How can I begin to live the life I want to live ideally?

3. *Become aware of your inner dialogue, as often as you possibly can.* Life gives you exactly what you expect. You write your own script in the drama of life, with every word you think and say — so it's up to you to write a better script for yourself.

4. *In a relaxed state, repeat the following affirmations, or formulas for success, to yourself:*

- I am unique. I have something to offer.
- It is my right and duty to be myself.
- I am becoming successful. I invite success and prosperity into my life.

- I attract the people and situations that will help me offer my service.
- Every day, in every way, I am getting better and better.

5. *At night, ask your subconscious to help you discover how you can be a complete success, make all the money you want, and serve humanity and the earth.* Fall asleep knowing that the answer already lies within you, and that you have already obtained what you asked for. The formidable power of your subconscious will work continuously, night and day, as long as you have steered it in the right direction.

Chapter 6

—ᨸ—

The Magic of Goals

*I resolved first to make enough money so
I'd never be stopped from finishing anything.*

— WILLIAM P. LEAR, Lear Jet Inc.

ONCE WE HAVE DISCOVERED OUR PASSION,
the field in which we want to succeed, we
can concentrate on fulfilling our plans. Some of the
best plans are the simplest. Thomas Peters and
Robert Waterman's *In Search of Excellence* discusses
the paradox of simplicity:

> Many of today's managers — MBA-
> trained and the like — may be a little bit
> too smart for their own good. The smart
> ones are the ones who shift direction all the
> time, based upon the latest output from
> the expected value equation. The ones

who juggle hundred-variable models with facility; the ones who design complicated incentive systems; the ones who wire up matrix structures; the ones who have 200-page strategic plans and 500-page market requirement documents that are but step one in product development exercises.

Our "dumber" friends are different. They just don't understand why every customer can't have personalized service, even in the potato chip business. They are personally affronted...when a bottle of beer goes sour. They can't understand why a regular flow of new products isn't possible, or why a worker can't contribute a suggestion every couple of weeks. Simpleminded fellows, really; simplistic even. Yes, simplistic has a negative connotation. But the people who lead the excellent companies are a bit simplistic.

To believe that we can make as much money as we want, to believe in our dreams, to disregard negative people, we need a good dose of naivete and simplicity. People who are too rational or intelligent can succeed, but their intelligence can limit the degree of their success, if it limits in any way the vast field of their dreams.

MAKE ONE CLEAR GOAL

People who don't succeed don't have precise goals. Any objectives they do have are, on some deep level, invariably low. They succeed at mediocrity or failure.

Some people don't even begin to set goals because of the overwhelmingly negative conversations they carry on in their subconscious. Almost all successful people started achieving their dreams only when they set clear goals and time plans for meeting them. (There may be some people who are exceptions to this rule — but we can't think of any at the moment.)

Set a precise goal, with a precise amount of income, and a time plan to make it. You'll discover that this is an important difference between those who succeed and those who don't. *We achieve what we plan to achieve, no more, no less.*

There is a story often repeated in business books about the salesman who could never sell more than $25,000 worth of his product in a month.

He was assigned to a territory where average sales were well below that amount, and he managed to sell $25,000 a month — quite an achievement for that territory. His manager sent him to a larger area where other salespeople were performing much better than that. His result: $25,000 a month. The dilemma he faced was clearly based on his goals and self-image. He didn't believe he could sell more (or less) than $25,000 a month, and his subconscious was set accordingly. This story is a good example of the power of the subconscious and the fact that we achieve any objective our subconscious sets for us.

Haven't your own experiences been directly linked to your objectives? Anyone with a vague, uncertain target — or no target at all — will get vague results, or no results at all. On the other hand, anyone who establishes a specific goal, backed with a specific plan of action, achieves it.

Why is this? The answer is within our subconscious mind: A clear target is the most simple and effective way of programming your subconscious. You won't necessarily have to work harder to achieve this goal; you might even have to work less. In the past, success has often been equated with long hours of hard work. But you'll soon find that when you align yourself with your purpose, release negativity, and program yourself for reaching your goals, you achieve results with less effort. It is possible to work less and get better results. A great many people know this is true. The secret lies in making a clear goal.

Even among the hardworking and success-oriented, a great many people don't have a specific objective in mind. Many people are satisfied with a slight improvement in their lives without ever considering or daring to set themselves a clear-cut figure that represents a *substantial* improvement in their lives, something that moves them toward the kind of life they *ideally* want to live.

What is your goal for next year? How much do you want to earn? $50,000? $100,000? $500,000? A million? If you want your lifestyle to improve substantially — a perfectly legitimate desire — ask yourself what goal you have to set. If you want a brighter future, establish your goals and determine how much time and energy you are willing and able to channel into reaching them. If all you can do is dream of getting a promotion or a fantastic job offer, but you don't have a specific objective, the "miracle" you are expecting will not happen. Your self-worth is exactly what you think it is.

Every successful person realizes this is an obvious truth: If you make a clear goal and begin to take the next apparent steps toward its realization — whatever steps are required to convince your subconscious you are serious about focusing on that goal — you will soon find you have reached it.

You Are Worth Much More
than You Believe

The greatest limitations people impose on themselves are created in their own minds. A person's worth is exactly what he or she believes it to be, no more, no less. Most people underestimate themselves, even if they appear self-confident. Those who know, deep down, that they are truly valuable are few and far between. Almost everyone has some degree of an inferiority complex, and this causes them to believe they are unworthy of success, of other people's esteem, or of much money.

The best way to increase your worth is to build your self-esteem. We have already presented techniques useful for bringing about fundamental change. One of the best ways of accomplishing this is to work with a specific monetary objective.

SETTING YOURSELF AN EXACT OBJECTIVE IS TRULY MAGICAL

Usually the first time you set yourself a specific monetary goal, you retain a certain amount of skepticism that limits the clarity and power of your ambition. So, make your first goals realistic; then, when you achieve your first goal, you can set yourself an even higher goal. Make this goal more of a *stretch*. Those who set themselves a clear target for the first time are generally surprised when they reach it and often go beyond it!

Challenge yourself to reach your goal. It's an exciting game that brings rewarding dividends. Perhaps you'll reach your goal in six months instead of the year you initially gave yourself. We've seen this happen many times. Setting yourself an exact objective is truly magical.

YOU ARE WORTH INFINITELY MORE THAN YOU BELIEVE

It's not an exaggeration — it's the truth: You

are worth *infinitely* more than you believe. The only problem is, quite possibly, no one has ever told you that before. Some people have probably tried their best to persuade you that the opposite is true.

Intelligence, work, motivation, imagination, discipline, and experience are, of course, important ingredients for success — but how many people do you know who have these qualities but still don't succeed, or don't live up to their full potential? Perhaps the same is true for you. Despite your obvious talents and efforts, success inexplicably escapes you. You meet people at work or at other companies who don't appear to be any more specially gifted than you, but yet they get the raise, the promotion, and achieve an enviable level of success. Keep this in mind: *Their self-images have determined their goals, which have determined their lifestyles.* And your self-image has determined your goals, which have determined your lifestyle.

Overcome your mental limitations and increase your self-worth by aiming as high as possible. It's not any harder for your subconscious to help you reach a higher objective than a lower one. And it's certainly much more enjoyable!

Make your goal a magnificent obsession.

Write it down in several places to keep it well in sight. Above all, keep it constantly in mind. A major principle ruling the mind is that *energy goes wherever your thoughts go*. By repeatedly thinking of your goal and making it a fixed idea, all your energy channels itself into helping you be successful. And thanks to the continuous work of your subconscious, circumstances and people will help you reach your goal in new and surprising ways.

MAKE YOUR GOAL A SINGLE, FIXED IDEA

A goal is like a magnifying glass. It focuses your energy on your target. Make your primary goal into a single, simple, fixed idea. This fixed idea not only allows you to increase your energy and level of success but also prevents a very serious mistake — scattering your energy. A fixed goal inevitably leads you to success.

The single-mindedness of a fixed idea also enables you to direct your professional and personal life more clearly, and with less effort. Everything that brings you closer to your goal should be encouraged. And you should let go of everything that distances you from it. How can you tell if something is bringing you closer or not? Your intuition will tell you in its usual way: a subtle feeling, a comment from a friend or partner, a phrase in a book or an article that resonates with truth for you.

Ask yourself for guidance, and you'll receive it. Create clear goals, and you'll achieve them.

SUMMARY AND RECOMMENDED ACTION

1. *Take a piece of paper and write down how much you'd like to earn next year.* When you have finished, consider this: When you created your goal, you based it on your self-image. Did you write down $40,000? If you did, that's what you thought you were worth. And you're right: You are worth exactly what you think you're worth. And when you can say $80,000 or $200,000, or a million, that's what you'll be worth. *You are worth what you believe you are worth.* And yet, your subconscious is unlimited, and so your potential is unlimited. It's true, therefore, that you are worth much more than you currently believe.

2. *Double the amount you wrote down a moment ago.* Assess your reaction. If you initially wrote down $50,000, why didn't you begin with $100,000? How

do you feel about this larger goal? Do you think it's completely far-fetched? Do you think that $100,000 is a lot? Too much? Many people would disagree with you. Each year, thousands of people become millionaires, and *millions* of people have yearly incomes far in excess of $100,000. They had enough of a positive self-image to aim for this income, and to go after it.

3. *In spite of what we've just said, don't set an overly unrealistic goal for yourself for your first year.* Do it step by step, but eventually make it ambitious. If you aim high and almost make it, you'll still have achieved a satisfying result. But if your target is low and you barely make it, you'll be disappointed and will have made very little progress. Set a goal that stretches you, and challenges your subconscious, but don't make it so high that it feels completely unachievable. Even though the goal-setting process is concrete and rational, the most important thing is convincing your subconscious that you're ready for this goal. You'll know it when you're ready; it will feel right, it will feel like a challenge you can't wait to take. Then the world will give you exactly what you ask for — no more, no less.

Chapter 7

A Plan of Action

*I believe the decision to focus your efforts is
extremely important, not only in the early days of
a company but later on as well.*

— DAVID PACKARD, Hewlett-Packard

THE MOST VITAL STEP ON YOUR PATH to success is preparing a step-by-step plan of action so that your intention becomes solidified, consciously and subconsciously. What actually unfolds may be quite different from your step-by-step plan — in fact, it *probably* will be quite different — but you'll reach the goal, nonetheless, soon after your intention is solid and unwavering.

Some jobs, unfortunately, will never bring great financial rewards; if money simply doesn't matter to you, so much the better. But if you want financial security and the means to pursue your dreams, change jobs, if necessary. Look for a position in a field that is compatible with your passion, talents, and skills, and offers a good salary as well. Or start your own business — in your spare time, if necessary.

No human being is infallible, not even the most experienced businessperson. Only those who do nothing never make mistakes. Even if you undergo temporary setbacks, you will still achieve your goals, provided your subconscious is properly programmed. This is the power of a precise monetary goal and a plan of action with a deadline.

Prepare a Step-by-step Plan of Action to Solidify Your Intentions

A step-by-step plan of action convinces your subconscious that your desire, your dream, your wishful thinking has become an *intention*. You intend to accomplish this goal, and create this situation in your life. The proof of your intention is your step-by-step plan. Convinced, your unlimited subconscious goes to work. You create exactly what you intend to create — no more, no less.

Applying your plan of action can mean taking risks that cause significant personal insecurity, especially if it's the first time you have set a goal and established a clear plan of action. Almost any change — even a change for the better — generates a certain amount of anxiety. Most people's need for security is so great that they are prepared to sacrifice their most precious dreams for it. Don't be afraid to forge ahead. You'll never regret it. We don't know of anyone who ever regretted taking a risk, when it was a step toward realizing a dream.

We recommend not to set more than two separate goals in one area of your life at a time. Pursuing too many goals at the same time diffuses your concentration and makes your work less effective. Pursuing goals in different areas of your life simultaneously, however, such as career, home, fitness, improved relationships, or finishing the next draft of your thesis or book is advantageous; each improvement benefits the other areas of your life.

Another highly beneficial action is to set goals for your future: one year, five years, ten, twenty-five, even fifty years into the future. Where do you want to be when you are sixty? What kind of person would you like to be when you are eighty? What kind of life are you dreaming of? How about your health and fitness? Do you want to have children?

What do you want to have accomplished? *Don't limit yourself.* Sit down and prepare a step-by-step plan.

We know many people who have written out a step-by-step plan for something, put it away somewhere and forgotten about it, and then discovered later they had fulfilled their plan, without even consciously thinking about it! We don't recommend this of, course — we recommend a healthy amount of repetition of your goals — but we have seen it happen many times.

You Are the Architect of Your Life — How Would You Like to Create It?

Disregard your present situation, your previous failures, your past. Forget about your age, as well. Many people well into their sixties and seventies know the best is yet to come. We can make our lives rich and full at any age. Often the dreams we nourish come true more easily than we expect — regardless of our age or current situation.

When you can picture yourself in an ideal future, when you know what you would like to do for the rest of your life, your short-term goals become far more clear and meaningful. You have a reason to get out of bed every morning and take steps that bring you closer toward fulfillment. You have charted the course of your life. You have become a visionary.

Picturing your life in this way — imagining your ideal scene — can literally shape your future, because through positive dreaming, through creative visualization, you program your subconscious. You flood it with images that are likely to come true. You hold the reins of command. You are indeed the architect of your life. Your blueprints are your goals and your ideal scene of your life in the future.

Your long-term goals not only define your ideal in life, they help to *create* it. They simplify many choices that would otherwise seem difficult or, worse still, arbitrary or absurd. When you don't know what you want to do with your life, it's difficult sometimes to make even the most insignificant day-to-day decisions. They don't seem part of a greater plan that gives meaning to your thoughts and actions.

Making a life plan is stimulating and motivating, and it contributes to success in all areas of life. Keep in mind, however, the need to remain flexible regarding the future, since life involves constant adaptation. What you are doing in five or ten years may not necessarily be what you expect — it might be much better than you ever dreamed possible.

When our minds are well-programmed, the situations that develop are always better than our previous situation. Every day, in every way, we get better and better. As we develop, our full potential becomes more and more realized, and the plans we dream up are bolder, more ambitious, more expansive. We often drop some of our initial plans along the way, usually because we were "thinking too small." As our self-image expands, our success in the world expands as well. We end up constantly progressing toward greater self-fulfillment — and personal enrichment, if that's one of our goals.

Now carefully plan your main objective for the next year — while still remaining flexible enough to respond to unforeseen opportunities that may very well come up. You'll have a clear picture of the work and effort you must put in to reach your goal. Divide your yearly goal into months, and then into weeks. Sound planning prevents a lot of worry and delay, and keeps you moving forward toward your goal.

CHARACTER EQUALS DESTINY

It is all well and good to set an objective — it is necessary for anyone wishing to be successful — but to try to work toward it day by day requires discipline. And the best discipline is the one we, and no one else, impose on ourselves. The Greek philosopher Heraclitus said, "Character equals destiny." If we look around at all the people we know, we see there are no exceptions to this rule. All successful women and men have strong character and are highly disciplined, each in their own way. No one succeeds without strength of character. To become our own master and take our destiny in hand, we need discipline.

By discipline, we don't mean a rigid schedule that excludes fantasy and relaxation. And we certainly don't mean workaholism. Discipline also means allowing enough time to rest, exercise, and properly nourish our bodies, enough time to meet family commitments, enough time for fun, enough time to be alone.

Overwork is never productive. Complaining of overwork is fashionable these days — and since most people don't use a tenth of their potential, they are overworked but never seem to accomplish much. They work too hard, and still lack discipline. They haven't created the habits that lead to success.

Success Is a Habit

Discipline and positive mental programming lead naturally to developing our own methods and ways of organization, discovering our personal working rhythm and patterns, and creating the habit of success. Until now, failure or mediocrity has simply been a habit. By replacing one habit with another, our new habit becomes second nature. Success is then irresistibly attracted to us.

The British writer William Makepeace Thackeray said it brilliantly: *"Sow a thought, and you reap an action; sow an action, and you reap a habit; sow a habit, and you reap a character; sow a character, and you reap a destiny."* These are words that have the power to change the course of our lives.

Summary and Recommended Action

1. *Take a piece of paper and write down what you would like to do with your life.* Add as many details as possible. What kind of work would you like to do?

How much money would you like to earn? In five years? In ten years? In twenty-five years? What kind of house would you like to live in? What kind of friends would you like to have? Will traveling be part of your life? Where will you spend your vacations? What about your family life? Write all of this down in as much detail as possible.

2. *Identify next year's objective.* Once you have your goal clearly in mind for the year to come, make a step-by-step plan to achieve it. Write down, in order, the things you need to accomplish. Set a date for each stage, and keep your deadlines in mind. And prepare yourself for some truly miraculous results.

Conclusion

—*m*—

Nothing in the world can take the place of persistence.
Talent will not: nothing is more common than
unsuccessful people with talent. Genius will not:
unrewarded genius is almost a proverb. Education will not:
the world is full of educated derelicts. Persistence and
determination alone are omnipotent.

— THOMAS WATSON, founder of IBM

THERE ARE NO "SECRETS OF SUCCESS." Almost all successful people enjoy sharing what they have learned along the way with those who are interested. We've certainly enjoyed writing this book, and telling you, as clearly as we can, not the secrets but the techniques, the practices, the knowledge, and the truths that have been instrumental to our success. The book is brief, but don't let that fool you: It doesn't take volumes to explain the powerful principles of success.

We can summarize them even more briefly:

• Imagine the life you want, and decide —

make an intention — to go for it.

- Discover what you love and make it your *vocation*. Vocation comes from the root word "calling." Find your calling.

- Devote your energy, your lifeblood, to your calling; the joy and fulfillment you receive generate even more energy.

- Know what you want; set clear goals with time plans for their completion. Turn your desires into intentions, and take the first steps toward achieving your intentions.

- Discover how to combine a clear intention — a single, focused objective — with nonattachment. Let your success unfold and grow with its own rhythm, in its own time. Have clear goals, yet don't become attached to results. Have clear objectives for the future, but live fully in the present, enjoying the present moment.

- Turn obstacles and past failures into an

impetus for success. Your failures have
given you the education you need to create abundant success in your life.

* Become an expert in your field. Always
  improve your skills and knowledge. Education is endless.

* See possibilities where others see only
  problems or impossibilities. Stretch your
  imagination. The world is full of infinite
  possibilities!

* Discover your own comfortable, natural
  working rhythm, your own form of discipline.

* Be persistent. The only real failure is giving up.

* Give back and give thanks. Give away at
  least ten percent of your income — and
  eventually much more, as you become
  more and more successful. The more you
  give, the more you will receive. This is an

infallible truth. You have the power to create a lot of good in the world for a lot of people.

• Live the life you want. Now. Keep reminding yourself that, every day in every way, your life is getting better and better.

Eileen Caddy, cofounder of the Findhorn community in Scotland, said it beautifully: "The secret of making something work in your lives is, first of all, the deep desire to make it work, then the faith and belief that it can work, then to hold that clear, definite vision in your consciousness and see it working out." That certainly sums it up precisely.

You have all the tools. Now it's up to you to use them.

ABOUT THE AUTHORS

MARK FISHER told a fictionalized story of his life in his first book, *The Instant Millionaire*. By studying with a mentor, he learned the principles of success he writes about in both that book and this one. He has interests in publishing and real estate, and lives in Montreal, Canada.

MARC ALLEN is co-founder and president of New World Library, a company that began twenty years ago as a start-up with almost no capital, and is now a respected contributor in the world of international publishing. He has written several books, including *Visionary Business: An Entrepreneur's Guide to Success* and *A Visionary Life*. He lives with his family near San Francisco.

REFERENCES

CHAPTER 1

Visionary Business: An Entrepreneur's Guide to Success by Marc Allen (New World Library, 1995)

A Passion for Success: Practical, Inspirational, and Spiritual Insight from Japan's Leading Entrepreneur by Kazuo Inamori (McGraw-Hill, Inc., 1995)

As You Think by James Allen (New World Library, 1991)

CHAPTER 2

The Fifth Discipline: The Art & Practice of the Learning Organization by Peter M. Senge (Doubleday, 1990)

In Search of Excellence by Thomas Peters and Robert Waterman (Warner Books, 1993)

Creative Visualization by Shakti Gawain (New World Library, 1978, revised in 1995)

CHAPTER 3

Global Mind Change: The Promise of the Last Year of the Twentieth Century by Willis Harmon, Ph.D. (Knowledge Systems, Inc. in cooperation with the Institute of Noetic Sciences, 1988)

The Seven Spiritual Laws of Success by Deepak Chopra (Amber-Allen Publishing and New World Library, 1994)

The Seven Habits of Highly Effective People: Powerful Lessons in Personal Change by Stephen R. Covey (Simon & Schuster, 1990)

CHAPTER 4

What They Don't Teach You at Harvard Business School by Mark McCormack (Bantam, 1986)

Made in America: My Story by Sam Walton (Bantam Books, 1993)

Living in the Light: A Guide to Personal and Planetary Transformation by Shakti Gawain (Nataraj Publishing, 1986)

CHAPTER 5

What They Don't Teach You at Harvard Business School by Mark McCormack (Bantam, 1986)

Work with Passion: How to Do What You Love for a Living by Nancy Anderson (New World Library, 1995)

The Fifth Discipline: The Art & Practice of the Learning Organization by Peter M. Senge (Doubleday, 1990)

The Seven Spiritual Laws of Success by Deepak Chopra (Amber-Allen Publishing and New World Library, 1994)

CHAPTER 6

In Search of Excellence by Thomas Peters and Robert Waterman (Warner Books, 1993)

New World Library is dedicated to
publishing books and cassettes that inspire
and challenge us to improve the quality
of our lives and our world.

Our books and tapes are available
in bookstores everywhere. For a
catalog of our complete library of fine
books and cassettes, contact:

New World Library
14 Pamaron Way
Novato, CA 94949

Phone: (415) 884-2100
Fax: (415) 884-2199
Or call toll-free (800) 972-6657
Catalog requests: Ext. 900
Ordering: Ext. 902

e-mail: escort@nwlib.com
http://www.nwlib.com